about Paths—Journeys Through Wonder, Danger, and Self:

People and Revelations of the Way

by

Robert Nichols

about Paths—Journeys Through Wonder, Danger, and Self: People and Revelations of the Way

by Robert Nichols
Copyright ©2017 Robert Nichols

Illustrated by: Robert Nichols

Mountain Muse Publishing
P.O. Box 406
Lincoln City, OR 97367

Print edition ISBN Number **978-0-9980910-9-9**

Contact Information

Robert Nichols / PO Box 406 / Lincoln City, OR 97367
MtMuse44@aol.com

MtMusePublishing.com

NOTE:

about Paths—Journeys Through
Wonder, Danger, and Self:
People and Revelations of the Way

and several other Robert Nichols' works,
are available as eBooks through a variety
of distributors throughout the world.
Also, most works are in the process of
being printed and published as printed
books-on-demand.

Robert Nichols' published works are listed in the section,
"Other Works by Robert Nichols" at the end of this book.

The Footlocker Series
"A Lifetime of Art"

about Time: Poems and Other Stories (2015)
about Mountain Living: Finding a Way (2015)
about Seasons: The Winds and Weather of Our Days (2016)

    On my seventieth birthday, my wife Carol presented me with the best gift I could have ever received.

    Over a period of months, she had undertaken the grueling task of excavating poems and essays and stories from my notebooks and yellow legal pads and grease-tinged napkins all stored in an old footlocker in the garage. Over fifty years of my scribbled beliefs and rambled passions, my devout exclamations of soul- and flesh-told instance, my art-blood observations of the world through which I pass—a trove of mad-sweet poems, ranting tirades, quirky philosophies; glimpses of bizarre beauty and mundane wonder—all transcribed from chaos to computer file.

It nearly killed her, but she would not be dissuaded. The dust, the terrible time-yellowed paper, the mold—allergy worsened to asthma but she would not stop. And her eyes—my handwriting is so bad I can barely read it myself, and the old typed pages are so faded—I would find her up in the middle of the night, hunched over stacks of the stuff with a bright desk lamp and a magnifying glass...

"Why?" I would implore.

Carol is not a morbid type. She has been my joy throughout these decades. But her reply was calm and chilling and true. "I have to get this done before I die. When we are gone that trunk will be tossed into some landfill and all of your work will be lost forever. I can't let that happen."

She kept most of it from me until my birthday. I suspected she might have recovered twenty or thirty poems from the rubble.

In fact, she presented me with a three-ring notebook containing 445 poems.

... and counting, there are well over five hundred now, most of which I had no clear recollection. New to me was the product of my life's work.

Such a gift. I am truly loved.

And *The Footlocker Series*? We decided the best way to preserve this work—these poems and essays and stories—and give them the only shot they may ever have at being read somewhere out in the world for which they were created, is to come up with a series of e-Books entrusted to cyberspace. Also, I am publishing them as printed books-on-demand.

about Paths: Journeys Through Wonder, Danger, and Self is the fourth book in this series.

Enjoy.
Every last word was written for you.

Dedication

To Carol
for
sharing my path.

I traveled these miles.
I wrenched these words from
the tangle of my days.

Carol,
with love
and belief
and
exhaustive toil,
in this Footlocker Series,
bundles
the works of my life
into sorted stacks
of heart and blood
and
gives order to the
chaos of my art.

Table of Contents

Paths

Paths—our journeys, the course of life decisions, the metaphoric routes we take from birth to this moment. Paths are defined by the experiences we have as we travel them—the places and people, the encounters, the discoveries. And, of course, our intermediate destinations and ensuing departures.

Regardless of where we wander, who we love or lose, embrace or fear—the profits and losses incurred along the way:

All the paths we have taken—they lead to now.

A word about the language in this work.

They Spoke with Filth and Beauty

I tell this the way I remember—
the events,
the conversations,
the epiphanies and doldrums
of the path.

And the truth
speaks sometimes
crudely.

And the way
can tell a harsh tale.

They spoke with filth and beauty,
rage and laughter.
I listened.
And I tell you these poems
and stories as they were.

The most angry of them
were the most vile.
The most humble
were the most kind of word,
kind of action.

I'll write it all.

Somewhere camping along the
Alcan Highway, writing the day's truths.
1985

Part I

The Travel Path

Sometimes it just seems like miles.

But then, as I read my notes and poems and thoughts from all these years and journeys, I realize this path of travel is miles, but, more so, it is people and nature and precious days—all upon the sacred subtlety of the highway of time ever-opening before me.

It seems I'm always writing about my travels. And now we put this book of gathered poems and essays roughly under the general heading of "Paths." It works. I'll start with some road words. *The Travel Path*, I call this. It's all a poem, all some allegorical attempt at saying what can only be felt in non-verbal heart shivers and visceral cringes.

And if we are not learning from the journeys, we're just ramblers going nowhere. It is not so much where we go as it is what we gain from the journey getting there.

I'll start with a trip I took in 1962 with my great friend Buddy French the summer after we graduated from high school. I was seventeen and thought it might be a good idea to get the travel bug out of my system before heading off to college that September.

Sure… some good miles, and I would be through with the road.

If You Don't Go Anywhere, You Won't Know Anything

No denying, I'm ready for a road trip for most any reason. When I was a kid, just sixteen and with a new driver's license, I was always more than willing to make runs down the hill to the Handy Dandy Market for a gallon of milk, a newspaper, a pack of Viceroy cigarettes for Mom—an emergency trip to the TV tube tester at the 7/11 to replace a vacuum tube or two and rescue the evening's two-channel array of *Maverick, Bonanza, Andy Griffith et al.*

"Give me the keys, Dad. I'll go."

Between high school graduation and the commencement of my less than stellar sojourn at the University of Richmond, my friend Buddy French and I decided to take a hitchhiking journey through the South. We lived south of Washington, D. C. adjacent to U.S. Highway 1, the old artery connecting the upper region of Maine at the Canadian border clear down the East Coast to the most southern reach of Florida at Key West. For the first couple of months of summer we talked about taking a trip. Unlike several of my friends, recent graduates of the Gar-Field High School Class of '62, I was only seventeen and too young to get a temporary job with the Government in D.C. I just did odd jobs and began a lifelong process of avoiding real money that has served me well right up to the present. It was never intentional, just the way my destiny has played out. Buddy, in the same fix with an August 18th birthday, had a low-pay, long-hours job selling fireworks at a stand on the edge of Bill's Shell Station down on Route 1. I would finish up my menial tasks doing gardening or day-construction labor or just sitting down in the basement playing my guitar and waiting for the call of what I was certain would become a significant life. It was a couple-mile hike from my home to the fireworks stand, but mostly downhill and Buddy usually had a car and would give me a ride back.

This was a few years before Interstate 95 was built. In the summer of 1962 the Richmond/Jefferson Davis Highway was a main route for traffic up and down the Eastern Seaboard—at least until it dwindled a bit through the Carolinas. Buddy and I would sit there talking about philosophy, religion, sex, art, sex and often we would dream of travel to places we had never been—like Key West, Florida, the finite conclusion of the conceptual wonder and allure of our hometown highway.

By mid-August, Buddy had saved enough money for college expenses and quit his job peddling pyro-fizzle and under-the-counter cherry bombs. I didn't have a job to quit. I just went to my father and asked for some money so Buddy and I could make a quick trip down to the farthest reach of Highway 1.

When my father was seventeen in 1932, the summer following his high school graduation, he had made a similar request of his dad when his friend *Buddy* Martin and he had dreamed up a trip from Oak Hill, West Virginia, to Washington, D.C.

So, when my dad heard my plan, he knew just what to say—the same thing his dad had told him thirty years earlier to the month. He gave me a ten-dollar bill and said,

"Robert, my dad told me, 'If you don't go anywhere, you won't know anything.'"

And, again, here's the rationale I came up with to support taking such a ridiculous and dangerous journey:
I'll take this trip and get all the travel out of my system before heading off to the serious challenges of higher education.

Right. As if the allegorical essence of the journey—this living metaphor of *the Path*—is a quantity to be expended.

No way. It turns out, trips are like Lay's Potato Chips with me—*betcha can't eat just one.*

And as to the specifics of the journey Buddy and I took—there were measurable elements of that trek down to the end of a highway like the size of the holes in my tennis shoes. And, of course, there were the "finite" mosquitoes that swarmed the dilapidated boathouse overhanging the backwaters of Key West where a barkeep lady had said we could sleep. The part of the journey that ended was a long run of pavement fraught and blessed with peril (some of those "good ol' boys" really seemed to enjoy the sport of attempting to run over hitchhikers), laughter (the small-town

Georgia speed traps), culture shock (racism as real as all the boasted tales of violent hatred of Blacks), a depth of exhaustion that tried flesh and friendship alike, and, of course, the end of an island and the commencement of the vast sea. What did not cease with our crossover from the southbound roadside to the north was this insatiable sense of wanderlust, the craving to travel on—the passion for each mile, for each boundless road dream, each day's new ground and new truth.

Why?

Travel is a metaphor for life. It's a path from where we are to someplace else, and... so go the epic and petty wonders that constitute the meaning to our days.

Notes from an Early Journey

I carried a small spiral notebook on the 1962 trip Buddy (Clyde Wesley French) and I took through the lush and swampy, kind and malicious, subtly poetic and bone-deep ignorant, two-laned heartland of the pre-Civil Rights Act of 1964 South. It was, as are all great journeys, life-changing.

In this message I wrote to my classmates years later, responding to a series of group e-mails concerning our 40th high school reunion, I mentioned what Buddy and I encountered in the "black and white" South back in those, supposedly idyllic days.

> … Someone sent a poem about the good old "black and white," *I Love Lucy*, God-'n'-Country days of our youth. I was just humming along with the words when I stopped and realized the utter nonsense of such platitudes.

> "Black and white" meant blind acceptance of the leaders who nearly ruined the nation with the sad fiasco of Vietnam. Think of the names of our brothers and sisters etched on black marble in Washington. Consider the whitewashed, so-called truth of those times and the belated regrets of the fool politicians who, in their reflective days just now, decades late, are beginning to admit maybe it was all just a big mistake.

> "Black and white" were the categories of separate-and-nowhere-near equal eating and drinking and learning establishments throughout the South in those *magical* days. In the summer of 1962, fellow graduate Buddy French and I hitchhiked down to Key West (just to see how far we could go on old U.S. 1) and we got a good firsthand look at what "black and white" really meant. In Richmond, capitol of the commonwealth of Jefferson and Washington etc., we stopped at an

ice-cream stand and there was a glass partition dividing the two service windows so that, by God, there was no way Black American citizens could possibly *contaminate* the cool white purity of our vanilla frozen custard. And it got worse as the long road meandered on down through the heartland of Dixie. I'll surely never forget the black-stained length of heavy pipe one self-proclaimed, latter-day *Johnnie Reb* pulled from under his seat as he roared us on down the narrow highway. "See that?" he said, just beaming with pride. "That there is Nigger blood."

"Black and white." Come on, let's admit it—did we really like Lucille Ball all that much?

It was a journey into the heartland of a troubled nation. As I said, I took notes and they tell of a difficult journey—at times grueling, physically and mentally exhausting; always a challenge. They are just sketchy details jotted along the way.

Just some examples:

Hitchhiking Trip from Woodbridge, Virginia, to Key West, Florida, 8:30 a.m., 8/4/62

1. Truck—South Hill, VA – Driving to ? (20 cents, food)

2. Station Wagon—from Conn., Near Apex, N.C. Very active—leaving wife, going to Australia.

3. Colored man, no teeth in front, watermelon truck—to Apex (food, 35 cents).

4. Straw Hat—Good Heavens, what a hick, to Tunstable Grocery—to New Hill.

5. Chevy Ranch Wagon—Big house—to near daddy-owned mansion, Sanford.

10

6. Colored man—classy—manner of speech—Dr.'s degree, to 15-501 cut off.

7. Banjo—55 Chevy.

8. Columbia, S.C.—Colored man—Conversation—Very enjoyable trip—push-button fancy Buick '47—shared peaches.

9. Convertible—2 mi.

   Warning Ticket *("Walking on wrong side of road" from Deputy Bubba)*—Stranded 4 hrs.

   ****

21. 2 Cubans to Islamorada—one here 8 mo. and other 2 mo.— Spoke of Cuba and hate of Castro, going back.
    Saw Everglades and ocean, beautiful green water, straight road.

22. Man to Marathon.

23. Couple with '46 Plymouth and air boat (avocado pears)—to Key West, Fla.—greatest disappointment of trip—full of bars, drunks, & rude women.

24/25. Rides by old car and drunk man.
    Spent night in boathouse on wharf behind Pier Bar.
    (airboat couple's place).

26. Ride to Naval Air Base—long hot day, hungry, miserable wait.

27. Ride back to Key West by sailor.
    Greyhound Bus to Miami (cold water at Bus Terminal)
    $4.60

    Walk part of way out of town then bus to outskirts – 55 cents.

28. Ride by New Yorker and sailors.

29. Rode in convertible to W. Palm.

30. Turtle hunters with wine.

****

46. Stood next to swamp—miserable because of gnats—short ride to outskirts.

47. Resident going to D.C. (in few days—enjoyed talk—many subjects) to Wilmington, North Carolina.

Slept couple of hours in small park (hiding from road).

48. Caught ride from Marine in fast (129 mph) car—to Jacksonville, NC (Camp Lejeune).

All night wait—sat in filling station—morning discussion with Buddy—flare up.

49. Long walk up the highway after Buddy—ride with bread truck—gave us rolls—reconnection with Buddy—to New Burn.
Walked across 2-mile bridge.

I'm including the whole batch of them in an appendix to this work—this list of short descriptions of the people who picked us up. A bit of commentary on the passing scene. Notation of money spent.

But they are much more than that. Collectively, they are a week's journey into being. I really can't tell you why these crude scraps are so important. But, on some primal level—the reason for the lives we live, the places we go, the people along our ways—it's a big deal

Read them. Know what a seventeen-year-old kid learned of the highway—of the path toward the rest of his life.

NOTE: Three poems and a related paragraph were written in my travel notebook as follow-up to the Key West trip in 1962.: "Next Year We'll go North," "It Was a Long Road," "Hitchhiking South." and "I Saw Life Yesterday."

Next Year We'll Go North

Next year we'll go north..
surely the mountains will be fresh, green—
reflecting sunlight in dew.

Next year we'll go north..
the air will be light.

Now we are wasting on the side
of an untraveled road,
our bodies beaten, our eyes weak—
the stars are scorning us in streaks and
blurs.

Next year we'll go north…

From *The Messenger*, Spring 1963, University of Richmond

It Was a Long Road

It was a long road.
It twisted and crawled through valleys.
It streaked through plains—
sometimes hot, humid, infested with a million flying,
swarming insects;
sometimes the wind was sharp—it cut through us
and we shivered and
sometimes all we thought of was home...
but we could not stop.

Now we are through—
content in the warmth of our meal;
safe in the softness of a mattress.
The mysteries of the winding,
unending road are
no longer.

Now: What have we learned?

From *The Messenger*, Summer 1963, University of
Richmond

14

A related paragraph:

Hitchhiking South

The gnats were invisible until they were stuck to your face and crawling in your eyes. They had seen the south from Washington to Key West and Route 1 was narrow and sparsely traveled—slow going through the Carolinas and Georgia. They had learned to hate Wadley, Georgia, for its ugly glares in a drug store soda fountain. And earlier they had seen the dew-glistening South Carolina morning green turn hot, smothering them. It was during a three-hour gap between small towns that he, with quasi-humor, had done his vicious dance upon the road map.

I Saw Life Yesterday

I saw life yesterday,
and yet…
no one listens—
and they just tell of the party,
the new girls,
the big laugh.

I saw life…
and yet

they don't listen.

I saw life and yet…

I really can't say.

From *The Messenger*, Winter *1962*-1963, University of Richmond

16

The Road Path Continues

Like I said, the idea of getting the rambling out of my system by taking that trip with Budcy in 1962 didn't work so well.

Sure, I went off to college and did some (a little) studying and all. But it really wasn't right for me. I actually enjoyed the learning—I always have. It was the tedium that seems to be requisite to college courses—the extraneous reading of books of flatline-dead prose, the droning lectures of minutia. That was part of it, I'm certain. But not all. The fact was: my spirit was restless and the highways were calling.

I wanted to get out there and start my lifelong poet's journey for real.

A Short and Serious Talk

After the first semester of my sophomore year had drifted aimlessly to a close in January of 1964, I dropped out of college for a year. That previous fall my father and I had engaged in one of our much-avoided serious talks. Certain that I would shatter his hopes and dreams for me in a scene of shame and disappointment, it had taken much gathering of courage on my part before I started the awful, thirty-second father-son encounter by sitting down on the couch across from where he sat in his big chair reading his newspaper. I said, "Dad, I need to talk to you. I've decided I'm not going to waste any more of your money down at Richmond. I'm going to quit school at the end of this semester."

To which he replied, 'That's good. I wasn't planning on wasting any more money on you anyway."

What a genuine relief that was. I didn't disappoint my dad after all—he had already written me off.

18

A Dream Actualizes

When I went to work at the railroad yard, I was a young guy with a little college and a big dream. I knew the hard and sometimes monotonous job was only an interim between school and either more school or, hopefully, some meaningful existence. For this reason, the long days of stacking boxcar after boxcar full of lumber into well-ordered piles were filled with thoughts and visions of distant ideas and places. The hours were packed with imagined vistas of green mountains and calling oceans. Young, it never occurred to me that the heads of many were forever numbed by dreams and more dreams and only dreams. But somehow I knew that to dream and never to act made dreams a poison in people's systems—a toxin that could make them sleep forever.

I was restless with unspoken sensations of self-entrapment.

Early in May the escape that I sought within myself came from an external source. McDuff, the boss who always wore a long black coat and who, at irregular intervals during the day, would sweep across the railyard like a charred, evil bird with a scowl on his face that was colder than the all-day drizzle and drifting wind, called me aside from a rising stack of lumber to tell me that he was going to lay me off. A chill of excitement ran through me and a rising pressure came up that took a vast amount of self-control, augmented by the sobriety of McDuff's demon-like appearance, to hold down. I wanted to explode into cartwheels and knee clapping, backslapping hyena laughing. But outwardly my figure spoke calmly of appreciating the job while it lasted and hoping to be recalled when work picked up again.

Now, I knew, was the time to act, to move. Now was my time to give action to the impotent, day-passing dreams. It was a Friday night and I said good-bye to my mother and father. I spent that night at my buddy Mile Daniels' house because he lived close to Highway 50 and I could get an early start from there the next morning.

Upon the way of my long hitching-hiking journeys I encountered most of the spectrum of human character from angel-sainted spirit guides, to unzipped fat guys with the wrong eye upon this lad, to the core of humanity who live epic tales of work and laughter and love. Good people, crazy people, every day folks, and a few who were truly evil. I was pretty much of an innocent boy when I set out from home in open-armed embrace of happenstance signaled by an honest smile and an up-pointed thumb. I was railroad strong, downtown wary, and free-verse poetic. What I didn't know of the real world was vast, dangerously so. But what I craved to learn was even greater.

Hitchhiking Trip
Washington, D.C. / Pacific Coast / Washington, D.C.
Commenced May 8, 1964

Saturday morning with an early May chill in the air. Standing on the gravel roadside of U.S. Highway 50 near Fairfax, Virginia, with a big silly grin on my face. The blue canvas gym bag that had portaged my sweat-laden clothes home and my clean ones back throughout my high school career in physical education, served now as the sole transport of my worldly goods: a couple of changes of underwear and socks; a clean shirt and pair of pants; a small notebook and a ball-point pen; my folding utility tool with assorted varieties of can openers, screw drivers, leather punches, eating utensils, a corkscrew, and one rather dull and extremely hard-to-find cutting blade; and various road maps. Along with a toothbrush and a Gillette Safety Razor, that was the whole kit for my journey.

I had $36 in my wallet.

I was ready. It was Saturday morning and I was on a west-bound highway with my thumb in the air and I knew that soon I would be rolling along with some complete stranger and I knew that no matter how far he was going I would be going farther. And I knew that I wouldn't be home for a while.

A '55 Chevy sedan slowed and edged off the highway. I ran to the side of the car and looked in. The driver was a middle-aged man who looked tired from a life of hard, heavy, unshaven work.

"Where you heading?"

"California."

Ever since I was a little kid the thought of going to California had intrigued me. My family lived in the vicinity of St. Louis, Missouri, and within a mile or two of that mystically alluring yellow brick road—U.S. Highway 66. I would listen to the people talking who had been out there and would wonder about how the real mountains with craggy tops peaked with snow, and the ocean waves pounding the base of cliffs would look like in person. Cowboy movies weren't so much bad guys and good guys as they were giant red rocks and giant canyons and giant deserts (and, of course, popcorn).

When I was fifteen my father was promoted and we moved to the suburbs of Washington, D.C.—another third of a continent farther from the dream.

Far more than a destination, *California* was a vision.

It was midafternoon and a series of several rides had brought me diagonally across the state of Virginia and to East-Central West Virginia on U.S. 60. I was riding in the back of a dilapidated pick-up truck with a country kid about my age. He nodded at the large angry-looking people riding in the cab.

With a sigh he said, "That there is my wife in the middle between my in-laws. We're just heading down the road a piece to pick up some stuff in Rainelle. Then we'll just head on back to their farm. Now, where did you say you're heading?"

I didn't have the heart to tell him.

"Just a ways past Charleston," I said.

As the truck ground and wound on, with my back against a bale of hay and warm sun shining down—the lush, almost tactile green of the mountains wrapped around me as we twisted through the valleys. The motion, the smells, the sounds, the immediacy of place and action—I had never known such a sense of freedom.

"You Ain't No Preacher, Are You?"

"You ain't no preacher, are you?"

"No!" I emphatically answered the beaked-nosed man. It was almost dark and the afternoon of long waiting and short rides had tired me, dimmed the morning's bliss and caused the ligaments of my thumb to stretch tight with a tinge of desperation with the passing of every car. When the little white Corvair halted its meteor-like motion in a dusty cloud, I lunged like a hungry, thankful puppy.

"Well if you ain't no goddamned preacher then get in. We've got a long ways to go." The little man spoke quickly as he vigorously spun the car back into flight. There was a blaze in the sound of his voice and in the look in his eyes and he was going a long way.

"It was a year ago, right there where you were standing, I picked up this young slick and as soon as he climbed in he started babbling." He mechanically picked up a pack of Pall Malls from the dash, lit one and covetously crammed the remainder of the cigarettes into his shirt pocket. "So, this guy starts telling me about how Jesus picked his ass out of all the masses of the world to spread the right stuff around to everybody. Well, I ain't one to knock a preacher or anything like that but this guy starts to really get on my nerves. Here I go and pick him up off the highway, just like you, and damned if he don't start telling me I'm gonna burn in hell if I don't listen to what he's got to say for Jesus and change my ways. How the hell's he gonna know what my ways are anyway, just seeing me for the first time like that?" There was an edge coming to his voice. He puffed heavily upon his cigarette and soon another was pulled from the shirt pocket located so close to his heart.

He sat quiet for a moment, the tiny white car hugging and straining at the curving West Virginia mountain highway.

Then exploding, "The son-of-a-bitch, after I went and picked him up off of this same goddamn dark, lonely highway, had the balls to tell me that I owed him three dollars and ninety-five cents for his goddamn precious Jesus-inspired time." The sharp features of the little man were taut. His words were sparks and his silence alive.

24

A moment of quiet. And then a sudden right angle jerk of his boney features—his burning eyes penetrating me, "What do you think about that?"

The longevity of this ever-precious ride resting on my reply, the fool-headed burst of my youth spat, "Well, as a matter of fact, Jesus and God himself dropped down the other day and said that you owed me one of your goddamned Pall Mall cigarettes!"

The little white car swerved and rolled through the curves as the quick little man convulsed with laughter.

The cool dark night rushing through the window surrounded me as I took a long drag on my new Pall Mall. (I didn't even smoke.)

Tired, and a little apprehensive I stepped out of the car (in Huntington, West Virginia) and bade my little friend goodbye.

Sleep in an Eroded Field

Huntington, West Virginia, like any other city in the dark hours of night, appeared to me in a yawn of blue neon-lit streets. Occasional blinking traffic signals marked the succession of a long series of intersections leading to the outskirts of town where I knew I would find my only chance at catching a ride.

But, perhaps stimulated by a tinge of fear, my groggy consciousness snapped to unusual acuity. The sound of my lone feet on the city sidewalk resounded. I found that I could stomp my feet and the whole night would come alive with the sound of me. I was the form of a single living man; treading through the dead sleep of thousands.

In the midst of my ego-inflated omnipresence, however, a cold realization seeped into me and soon quelled my exuberance. Not only was I the sole performer in this theater of slumber, also, I was the sole prey of the never-sleeping evil that hovers forever in the slanted shadows of the alleyways.

Hushed and humbled, I crept, clinging to the synthetic leather strap handle of my blue canvas gym bag.

Huntington is not a large city and soon the course of my highway became a boulevard with driveways leading to snug-looking houses full of sleeping rooms and sleeping people. And, with the ambience of home-like suburbia, my fears were daunted in an inundating rush of weariness. I knew soon I would have to stop for what was left of the night.

It was clear to me that an alien sleeper in this world of security would be bitterly unwelcome. Though, inwardly the sights and impressions of my childhood spoke, "This is home. This is the place to lie down and rest myself, this is the place where the night is kind." I sensed that I had made my home where no person would see me, where only I would rest.

I walked beyond the blue streetlights with the stretching, sleep-hazed halos around them. I walked beyond the pavement of sidewalks, and beyond the well-ordered canopy of well-ordered trees. I walked beyond the block-strong squares of well-ordered houses.

And there, in a neglected eroded field, shadowed by the glare of an all-night filling station, I slept.

Inching and Quarter-Inching Across Eastern Kentucky

In the gray of early morning I awoke. Glad to see the warmth of day sifting through the shivering misery of my bed-less night, I stiffly walked to the highway. I had decided, sometime during my sleep-spotted stay in the vacant lot, that not only would it be enjoyable but also it would be damn comfortable to spend my next night in the comfortable abode of my brother John and his wife Tonie. John was stationed at Fort Knox which is located about twenty miles south of Louisville, Kentucky, and I figured that with a reasonable amount of luck I would reach there by early evening.

A few local rides and I was casting a sun-lit shadow down the highway just west of Ashland, Kentucky. These rides, though they were short, were not easily come by. There was a good deal of walking and waiting between them and by the time I was through Ashland the morning was too warm.

The sense of liberation that I had felt the day before was gone. I noticed this change soon after I'd started down the highway that morning and had encountered difficulty in getting a ride—the same difficulty that a day earlier hadn't bothered me. This bliss-daunting wave of impatience became more intense as I stood by the near-silent highway west of the city. The semi-rural, spring-verdant countryside had become simply the faded background of a black asphalt, yellow-lined strip of conveyance between two predetermined points. The sounds and smells of these minute but all-existent specks of life were dulled by my focused attention to the prospect of the sound of an approaching automobile. The concerted effort of a thousand birds, bugs, and wind-rustled leaves was degraded to an irritating hum behind my mental computation of miles and hours between myself and Louisville.

Slowly, painfully the East Kentucky farmers and salesmen and their sons inched and quarter-inched me through the rolling green of their land. My schedule of distances, and hours, and arrival times, and, "Hello John, thought I'd stop by," fell prey to modification after modification as my impatience grew. The afternoon was waning when my stalling fortune brought me to Lexington.

Walking through Lexington, with the pained prospect of more than sixty miles to Louisville and Fort Knox beyond that, and with more than thirty-four of my original thirty-six dollars intact, the allure of a Greyhound Bus terminal was more than I could stand.

It was dark as the giant bus cleared the city and comfortably moved onward toward Louisville. Sitting back in the large tilted seat with all the worth of central Kentucky blurring by me, with the security of a ticket all the way to Fort Knox bought and securely held in the bosom of my shirt; I considered the value of my day.

I thought back to remember where I had been and realized that I had been nowhere; I thought back to remember who I had met and realized I had met no one; I thought back to the reason for my leaving and realized that I was nowhere.

The bus from Louisville down to Fort Knox was filled with guys about my age heading to basic training and their first weeks of military life. The bus was pierced with the sounds of jovial nervousness. As the tense laughter and grumbling complaints persisted, the relatively quiet figure sitting next to me murmured, "You wouldn't believe, from the sounds of it all, that half of these bastards volunteered just like me."

And as I snugly relaxed between the soft white cleanness of my brother's guestroom sheets, I quietly knew that my precious feelings of freedom could only come from a delicate balance between going to a somewhere that had no name; and staying just ahead of a nowhere that could follow me wherever I went.

After spending a day and another night at my brother's house I was again standing impatiently by the highway. The impatience that churned within me was not like that which I had experienced earlier. This was not rooted purely in the demands and destinations, in the relationship between the hours of a day and a thin line on a map.

No. Something much more powerful was a-light.

A Girl in Southern Missouri

The weeks of hours and the months of days that I had toiled away at the railroad were not filled solely with thoughts of travel and philosophical notions of life's journey.

There was a girl.

Beyond the furtive and physical encounters of scattered weekends; beyond the ear-shattering sounds and blurred shapes inhabiting Washington bars; beyond the bubble and waste of drunken eyes—there was a girl.

Carol was the girl who had lived a couple of streets over from me all the way through elementary school and up into high school until my family moved to Washington. She was my sister's best friend. She was my buddy and her mother trusted me. Carol flew to Washington two times to visit us. We wrote numerous letters. I loved her and now she was going to college in Cape Girardeau, Missouri.

"I'm heading for Cape Girardeau, I know a girl who is going to the college there and I thought I would stop off there for a couple of days."

The driver gave no immediate response to my reply. We had been riding for several miles and I had been subjected to a slow, deliberate interrogation about my whereabouts, my yesterdays, and tomorrows. I had been cautiously honest in my replies for, today of all days, rides were desperately needed.

Appraisingly he stared at me for a moment out of the corner of his eye. Then... "Well, you're in luck, buddy, I'm heading for Cape Girardeau myself." The relief and exuberance that I felt must have been obvious. The stern boundaries of his sunbaked face cracked into a good smile.

I spent five beautiful days in Cape Girardeau. The mornings I wandered around the small Mississippi River town, or lounged on the warm grass lawn of the campus. Carol's classes were scheduled such that by eleven-thirty she was through with school for the day. I would sit playing the radio in Carol's car until ten. At that hour the local station began their daily custom of broadcasting the names and addresses of everyone who had either entered or been released from the city hospital. By then the grass was dry and the groundskeeper, armed with his spear, was usually walking somewhere near me, mumbling and grumbling slightly as he plunged the tip of his weapon into scattered paper cups and beer-can debris.

The old man was always ready to talk and all our conversations began with his fevered denunciation of litterers chorused by my shaking head and ready approval of all that he said. We didn't talk of world crisis or integration, the price of food or war escalation; we talked of things that I don't remember and those the sunny warm mornings in the park waiting to see the girl I loved still hover in my mind as pleasant times.

My sleeping accommodations during my stay in Cape were not so plush as at my brother's house but, compared with the hard cold clay of a vacant lot, they were more than adequate. Carol's car was a small green-and-white Rambler affectionately named "Sweet Pea." I slept in the front seat which was slightly larger than the rear. Assuming a semi-fetal position with the excess length of my legs hanging to the floor beneath the steering wheel, I did okay. (It was a couple of years later that I realized the seats fully reclined into sleeping position in the old Rambler.) The nights were long but at least they were warm and when Carol would burst from her dormitory cage early in the morning with a pitcher of cold water, a few scraps of bread scrounged from the food caches of her fellow inmates; and, mixed with concern for the stiffened state of my body, a look of honest joy in seeing me, I knew a bed of nails would have more than sufficed.

The portion of my day that streaked from the time that I picked Carol up after her last class, to her twelve o'clock curfew is shrouded in indistinct remembrances like the song of wind chimes. After I picked up Carol we would go to the A&W Root Beer Stand and there one day she told me, "All I can give you is love and cheeseburgers." The five days were blessed in the wonder of two people in an afternoon, two people in an evening.

She drove me to the outskirts of town and it wasn't in the early, ambitious hours of the morning. It was in the early, reluctant hours of the afternoon when the tear-eyed girl pulled away from the gravel driveway and headed back toward town, leaving me a hollow, lone figure beside the highway.

A Hard Road Onward

Rides were slow in coming and, the way I was feeling, discouragement came easily. That whole slow-moving afternoon was filled with the temptation to shift from the northbound, St. Louis side of the highway to the southbound, back-to-Cape Girardeau side. I finally caught a ride through to St. Louis with a real loser.

When the old Cadillac pulled over to the side of the highway, I experienced the first ray of optimism that the day had offered. The car bore California license plates and surely anyone from so far away would certainly be going at least as far as St. Louis. The ragged old car slowly but persistently gained speed until the green Missouri countryside became only a potentially, pain-evoking barrier to be avoided by desperately hoping that the maniac driver could stay on the curving road. The great mass of the once pompous automobile would lean heavily and I'd feel the muscles of my legs and feet grow tense. The wild-eyed driver, in his madness, seemed oblivious to any danger. But then after a hundred curves something happened—the old Cadillac, as if its proud spirit had finally been broken, sputtered and coughed and mournfully ceased to run.

As the dead car coasted lazily down a hill and into the lot of a conveniently located gas station, the fire left his eyes and he turned to me and said, "Well what the hell kind of mileage you expect out of her, we're heading straight north and that's as uphill as you can get."

As I sat there numbly reacting to his statement, he opened the back and started rummaging through a pile of assorted used automobile parts strewn upon the floor. The thought of being stranded any longer on this highway just short miles from Cape and Carol was so distressing that when the driver was through bartering his obviously stolen merchandise for a few gallons of gasoline, I remained in the car. I would ride with this fool because getting to St. Louis and a highway heading west was more than a need, it was a necessity.

"Say, uh," he mumbled as we roared and rattled onto the highway, "you got any money, fella?" I'd been halfway expecting this plea ever since I climbed into the car and noticed that the gas gauge was near the empty line. And by then I had decided that the money for gasoline that would get us to St. Louis would be more than worth the couple of days' food that it would have otherwise purchased.

He started a long rant and whine about his miserable bad luck and I just watched the miles as they sped north.

"The son-of-a-bitch only gave me four gallons for that regulator. It was worth five dollars easy. That won't get us more than half the way to St. Louis and I gotta go to Chicago cuz my mother is sick and maybe she's gonna die and I gotta get there so's I can see her. I had plenty money when that bastard fired me and I started from California. Plenty money to get here and maybe I'd be eating steak and buy you one too, but damn I got all messed up and got way down in Texas somewhere and I've been driving for five days and I ain't but just got out of Texas. I had plenty money but them bastard Texas cops went and took a bunch away from me. I was doin' okay and I found my road back that went to Chicago and I was just drivin' like I am now and them bastards pulled me over and took a whole bunch more of my money and goddamn if they didn't just go and do the same thing again not more than about an hour later and then I didn't have no money at all left hardly and we ain't never gonna make St. Louis on that damn few gallons that bastard give us." His eyes squinted half closed under the weight of his deeply wrinkled forehead. "If only I didn't get in all that trouble with them damn police down in Texas. I'd of had lots of money now. We wouldn't have no trouble at all gettin' to St. Louis then. If only them coppers had left me alone I'd be okay now."

And after I bought him two dollars' worth of gas he didn't let up on his grumbling and when I left him at a St. Louis filling station bartering for more gas, his forehead was still wrinkled and his mind still full of "ifs."

34

The Exterminator

It was dark and I was sitting in a tavern drinking beer with a man who was on his way to his job working a night shift at a factory down the road. I was *Smalltown*, Missouri, in a large hollow building and there were just three of us: the lady behind the bar, the factory guy, and me. The bar-lady said the place really filed up with dancing and music on a Friday or a Saturday night. I was feeling okay then, the beer tasted good, the guy was paying for it, and the factory road was still fifteen miles farther west and the three of us laughed loud enough to fill the emptiness of the old building.

I was cold, a little bit high, and absolutely alone in the darkness of a quiet highway. My new friend had left me there an hour earlier and not more than a half a dozen cars had passed me since then. The agony of the day was returning to me. Thoughts of Carol and questions why the hell was I heading for California when she was in Cape Girardeau were troubling my mind. The soft remembrances of feelings of the previous days were tearing at my will to go west, my will to go anywhere but back to Cape.

But I knew going back would be a disastrous move.

It was close to eleven when I got a ride.

"Howdy," said the hand-shaking figure in the covered pickup truck. "My name's Marvin Sterninbarker—I'm an exterminator. I've traveled all over this damn country just going to the doors and saying, "I'm Marvin Sterninbarker the Bugman, Ma'am, got any bug trouble?' There ain't a place in this country that there aren't people who have heard of me. Where are you from? Virginia you say, well I've got lots of friends in Virginia and lots of people there can tell you about me. I've bugged down in Florida and all the way up into Washington state and across at Kalamazoo and in old El Paso—and there ain't nobody forgot old Marvin either, if I went to any of them places they'd still know my name."

Marvin had the look of someone who, in most cases, was probably just remembered rather than remembered and liked. He had a thin smile and hollow-staring eyes that constantly seem to be looking at your body. His voice was almost shrill and was quick like his eyes. He shook hands like someone who had read in a book that a firm handshake was the key to success and a sign of masculinity. I hadn't trusted him from the time that he'd said, "Howdy."

We drove for about a half an hour, Marvin expounding upon his wide notoriety and vast amount of travel the whole time, when he decided that he'd like to shoot some pool and, though it had been several years since he had been in Missouri, he thought that he remembered a late-night tavern about a mile up the road that had a pool table. Some of my suspicions about the validity of Marvin's claim to fame were elevated when we walked into the bar, picked up pool cues, and the bartender impassionedly said, "How's the bug business, Marvin? I ain't seen you for couple of years."

As I had suspected, Marvin wasn't very far along on his second beer before he developed a definite irregularity of gait as he moved around the pool table. And it wasn't long after he started on his third that the sweetness of brotherly love overcame him and he grandly offered me a partnership in his globe-encompassing enterprise. "I'll make you the best damn bug man in the whole goddamn country!"

After allowing a proper interval to pass, at least ten minutes, to enable Marvin to forget the generous offer that he had made me, I mentioned that the time had come for me to depart his company. Marvin, returning his beer bottle to the table abruptly, declared, "I'll drive you twenty miles to the junction!"

About twenty or thirty minutes after we left the tavern, without passing any sign of conscious life the whole way, we came upon a lone car along the side of the oncoming highway that had apparently had a flat tire on the right rear side. Standing beside the car, almost in the road and clearly in the direct scrutiny of the bug-truck headlights, was the magnificent form of a tightly-clothed female.

Marvin immediately applied the brakes and slowed.

From the look in Marvin's dashboard-lit face, I felt that a word of caution was in order. "Say, Marvin, you'd better watch what you say to her, her boyfriend might be around somewhere."

With an impulsive glance, Marvin quelled any further attempts that I might have made to stay his approach to the seemingly solitary girl. We squeaked to a stop and, rolling down the window, Marvin grinned hungrily at the helpless damsel as she approached his side of the truck.

"Hiya, Baby, anything I can do for ya?" His right hand dropped from the steering wheel and onto his lap, his words were hot, and they sounded like they were full of slobber. He lustfully leaned out the window toward the blinking-eyed girl when, slowly and with menacing stride, a giant boyfriend figure emerged from the dark side of the disabled car. I was certain the doom of the night was about to befall me. The figure approached and as he did he produced a flashlight which he beamed directly into my stunned companion's face.

Then, suddenly, the giant figure rolled his ferocious head back and howled with laughter. As he recoiled from the force of his burst and fell almost fully upon the hood of his car he was able to gasp out the words, "Goddamn, it's only Marvin Sterninbarker!"

Just Some Good Ol' Boys

It all became suddenly, surreally threatening.

I had gotten way off the main road.   It was late afternoon and I was desperate for a ride when a car full of crazy-looking filthy people stopped. I thought about passing up the offer but I'd been there a couple of hours and figured it was worth taking a chance just to get moving again.

Crushed in the middle of the front seat by sour-smelling fat guys with swinish faces and twanging words of threat and hatred, as we careened through the back country the talk of the men in the seat behind me became increasingly violent. They were all passing around a big jug of some kind of yellow-white wine. No one offered me a swig and soon it became obvious the plan was to kill me and dump me in a ditch.

"How's about now, Tommy?" asked a whining voice from just over my shoulder.

"Oh, I don't know, Butch. It could be kinda messy in the car."

And how they all laughed. I was trapped and scared and sure as hell they were going to kill me.

"Wanna see my ball-peen hammer, Boy?" taunted the voice of Butch, who was seated just behind my fragile skull as he repeatedly popped it sideways into the palm of his hand.

There could be no escape. Wedged in by the sweat-soaked girth of my captors, my only hope was to distract their blind wrath.

The driver was handing the bottle across to the passenger on my right when, out of some survival instinct, I grabbed it out of his hand and saying, "I didn't think you boys were ever going to offer me a drink," I took a long guzzle of the sickening sweet wine and passed it on. The murderous band was stunned by my affront but then, with wheezing laughter and much slapping and "I'll-be-damning," hostility melted away into a bond of drunken brotherhood and I was saved.

At the edge of the backwoods they left me off with hoots and blessings, made a U-turn and disappeared. I thought of their hacking coughs and scabby lips and the sticky mouth of that communal jug and spat for hours.

You know—just some guys out for a little Saturday afternoon lynching.

Kansas and the Wind

At my first sight of the vast flat spread of Kansas that lays west of Topeka, I felt a sense of liberation like I had known while passing through West Virginia on the first day of my trip. The warm sun and the limitless green of the spring grain all around me alive in the wind made me laugh out loud and kick at the rocks at my feet and think "Damn, look where I am."

I leaned lazily against the wooden post of a highway sign and pulled my slightly used bag of Bull Durham cigarette tobacco out of my shirt pocket by its yellow pull-string. As I said, I wasn't really a smoker but I did get a kick out of assembling an occasional cigarette. I withdrew a manila-colored sheet from my orange package of Zig-Zag, wheat straw, gummed edge, cigarette papers." The famous Kansas wind was too much of a challenge for an amateur cigarette-roller like myself to ignore. I turned so that my body shielded the operation but, just as I finished pouring the right amount of tobacco onto the paper, the wind perceived my threat and swung around to my side, scattering precious flakes of Bull Durham. Undaunted by the initial failure, I quickly spun my back to the wind and dumped an extra-large hump of tobacco onto the awaiting crease of the proudest product of the Zig-Zag company. But, again, my adversary shifted and countered my assault. It was no longer just a casual game. The first two attempts had so depleted my supply of tobacco I realized the next try would have to be an all-or-nothing proposition. The only possible course that had any hope of success was a mass deployment of the remaining contents of the bag. The wind backed off, hovering at a menacing slow idle, and I, seizing the opportunity, spun and showered the thin paper with the totality of my golden-brown flakes. The wind reacted rapidly and dashed at my sides. The air was, for a moment, filled with the scattering of fine-cut tobacco. I vigorously rolled my fast-diminishing pile, as the force of the wind pitched me to and fro. I turned evasively and the wind grew furious. As I licked the gummed edge and began to even the tobacco within the paper tube, the angry wind, perceiving that this would be its last chance to defeat me, summed its force into a huge gust that clouded the air with dust and tobacco and thrusted me heavily against the sign post.

The warm Kansas sun flamed high above, the rustling green of the infinite fields ceased moving, the light-colored cloud of dust settled slowly back down to the side of the highway, and I stood proudly in the stilled air. The final assault of the wind had been too late and in defeat my noble challenger had humbly retreated. Once again, victory was the taste of a cigarette.

The way through Kansas.
Unguarded along the road—
playing games with wind.

Yes, I learned of fatigue and threat and humor—patience, persistence, and play—but from the Dogman, I learned of evil.

The Dogman

And the Dogman, even among the most perverse and cruel along the travels of my youth—the Dogman the worst of them all.

It was mid-morning when the dog trainer picked me up along with a couple of six-packs of beer and headed west from the city for the two hundred miles out to Hays. I was relieved that the gruff man offered me none of the beer. I'd had enough of drink for a while and was glad to take in the view with a clear head. And, also, I sensed danger in this squat and squint-eyed man and knew I must be cautious. I had encountered the ignorant filth of a dozen varieties of human vermin along the road, but almost immediately I knew this man was truly wicked.

The large vehicle was stacked full of cages stuffed with cowering hulks of canine fur and smelled of urine.

About halfway through the first six-pack, the taciturn man suddenly got hit by a buzz and started spewing his sordid truths. In a flurry of vitriol, he cursed all the non-Caucasian races of mankind, all the politicians who ever packed a suitcase and headed out to Washington, and with particular ire, all the women who had ever denied the clutch of his clammy hands. Seasoned by the ways of the highway, I said nothing in defense of Indians, Mexicans, Blacks, or of Franklin Delano Roosevelt and John F. Kennedy. However, I could barely stifle my repugnance when the twisted rage of the man described women. When he said "cunt" I shuddered—by God, the scummy bastard was talking about mothers and sweethearts, Mother Teresa and Amelia Earhart and Jackie Kennedy and, damn him, this low-life slime defiled my own mother and Carol, the love of my life. But I said nothing. With wisdom often comes silence.

This man beats dogs, I thought.

And then it got worse. Popping another can of beer the Dogman started laughing and telling terrible stories of his adventures with his best buddy, Petey. "Me and Petey, man, we've taken down a few

Niggers along the way." He reached under the seat and revealed the grip of a large pistol. "See?"

The situation was getting worse and there would be no escape until the fiend turned from my highway and the ride was over. Then he told about how he and Petey had gotten really drunk a couple of winters earlier and grabbed a young girl—"sweet thing she was, too," and had taken her out in the winter woods and... "Hell, we was just screwin' the little bitch in a snowdrift and I don't know if she just got too cold, or just got too scared but damn f she didn't die right there with Petey workin' away on her."

And then, realizing he had sa d too much, he said no more and the chill of his quiet was terrible.

At Hays the ride was over. ' It gets flatter and flatter to the west. There are stretches of Eastern Colorado that don't have no edge at all—just go on and on. You'll see. Eastern Colorado's so damn wide and flat there ain't no place to hide, Boy. No place."

The words of the despicable man are as real as I can recall of a truly unforgettable experience. I still think about the pretty young girl, the stinking rapists, the bitter-cold snow. I yet recall the sense of repulsion, the chill of fear at the deepest realization of evil that I had ever known. He could still be out there somewhere—old and wicked and, with rasping, sour breath, muttering his wicked tales to any who are damned to listen.

43

The Rubber-Man

A good man picked me up somewhere along the Kansas highway and drove me hours westward into the expanse. He was a traveling condom salesman out to save farmers' daughters from their fertility and farmers' sons from rutting repercussions—not to mention protecting them from all manner of traveling-salesman-transmitted diseases. I called him a hero and he appreciated the praise. It was good laughter, good talk, but then it got dark.

You see, as you travel west across the plains it just gets flatter and flatter and bigger and, eventually, you just have to laugh at how ridiculously wide and forever it gets.

"Man, this is some kind of country you've got out here." I said.

"I know."

And we both laughed—the Trojan prophylactic salesman and the trekking poet-boy—laughing at the immensity of Gods and the insignificance of men, I guess.

"It's kind of the reason I picked you up today. I know it's not the smartest thing to pick up hitchhikers—hell, you might murder me and take my case of rubbers."

"It's a thought."

"You think I travel these lonely stretches unarmed?"

"Okay. You're safe this time. Besides, with my luck I'll almost never have use for the damned things anyway."

"Hey. Buy a three-pack, change your luck."

"I've carried the same rubber in my wallet so long it's left a permanent oval dent in the leather."

Humility brings out the truth in people more than bragging and lying.

"So, I took a chance on giving you a lift because of this damned big country and because I've got to travel into the night. I love it out here, but, sometimes, about dusk and then into the darkness—it isn't such a good place to be alone."

And on the evening following the afternoon of the Dogman, I knew much of what could be the threat of darkness.

As a lone traveler, I knew well the chill, the insecurity, the primal trial of dusk.

"And," he continued, "you're about to get a good sense of just how big and dark this country can be. I've got to turn off up here in about an hour. I'm going to leave you right in the middle of the biggest bunch of nothing in all of America."

And thus it was. He pulled off the road, shook my hand, gave me a three-pack for the road, and disappeared down the southbound highway toward Lamar, Colorado. (Come to think of it, I believe somewhere in a box of artifacts from the fifty-years plus since that night, I might still have those Trojans—so much for improving my luck.)

This was before the Interstate Highway System was nearly completed. It was a two-lane highway and there were long intervals between passing cars. There were stretches with no distant headlights approaching; no dimming taillights departing. No light at all and the stars were cold companions for this lad.

This boy, frightened and excited to a shiver, had gotten exactly what he was seeking, what I still seek: the raw-edged wonder and threat of mortal experience.

Denver...

A series of rides left me off in Limon, Colorado, at the junction of U.S. 40 and U.S. 24. The sun was gone and the sky was a dry, tired pink. I stood next to the Denver sign and in the quiet listened to the wind-blurred sounds of the dusk. An hour of futility—cars and headlights and *then* the inevitable self-inquisition—doubts, questions, yesterdays, tomorrows... I sensed a pattern in my moods. Fatigue was hell on belief.

Joy is a fickle damned thing when you give your fate over to the whims of high-speed strangers flying past you through the night.

Just a dip into the ever-hungering maw of despair and, at last, a ride with a wild-haired, sailor-voiced, tattooed savior—the blessing of a blaspheming bullshitter who gave me some fine miles and a trip to Denver. Thank you, Sailorman. I'll believe all your lies and never forget you.

Denver came strong and fast and bright. We skirted downtown to the north and as we neared his exit he told me I'd better go up to Wyoming because Colorado was strict with its hitchhiking laws. And then, as he pulled onto the exit ramp, I laughed as he told me one last tale about the bellybutton ornament of a dancer he had met in Turkey. And I laughed and laughed and stepped out of the car and my smile became crisp as it met the void of the street.

"How do I get to Highway 40?"

"It's one hell of a long way south of here," said some gas station guy.

I think it was Wadsworth Boulevard—one of those north-south grid roads on the west side of the city. Walking and seeing the now-familiar sight of hundreds of red taillights streaming before me in the direction that I was traveling. I walked through the parking lots of laundromats and drugstores and driveways and saw the numbered blocks creep from 70s on down toward my goal: the zero block of Colfax Avenue. I had been promised by the voice of dreams that Denver would give me mountains and the night had stolen them from me. It wasn't all bitterness though. The day had given me a choice and in the night boulevards, Denver, cool with evening's air, told me good things in twinges of optimism. Being dead tired was nothing. Being alive, now that was something.

Soon my weariness ceased being a form of martyrdom and became a badge of individuality in the mass of swarming, smug comfort.

Somewhere along there I caught a bus. I thought, seeing the ordered sprawls and congestion of the old "Queen City of the Plains" that Denver must have been the first place where cowboys died forever.

Colfax Avenue. Look at me you dead cowboys.

Colfax, like the sounds and shapes of any city, was neon and clutter but the best thing it did was go west. And west was right into the fourteen-thousand-foot wall of the Rocky Mountains.

Too bad it was dark.

I walked for many blocks ther a boy and a girl picked me up in a tiny little car and took me out far enough that the traffic wouldn't all be local and I would have a chance at catching a ride across the mountains. In a way, I wanted to save my first encounter with the Rockies for daylight but at the same time knew to linger in Denver very long would mean a couple of dollars for a hotel room and besides, it was an exciting idea to think of climbing half way up the black sky.

But all the night's illusions were shattered later as I, leaning nervously toward the opened window of the patrol car, was officially warned of the fate of hitchhikers in Colorado and directed to a city bus stop where I could buy a ride downtown to the Greyhound Bus Terminal.

What was it Sailorman told me about going north to Wyoming? I remember wondering if the story about the bellybutton ornament was also true.

47

The Bus to Cheyenne

I took an isolated seat in one of the rows of hardwood pews that filled the center of the terminal and, echoing about the large building was the slurred rollcall of the nation.

"Limon-Bulington-Colby-Wakeeney-Hays-Salina-Mahattan-Topeka-Kansas City-Columbia-St. Louis-boarding Gate Three."

It was eleven o'clock at night and the Cheyenne, Wyoming, bus didn't leave until four. This night had settled and sleep was a beautiful thought. With the three-dollar ticket in my pocket, I was legally deserving of all the slumber that I could render from the harsh wooden bench. This was serious business for me. On more than one occasion at the terminal in Washington, D.C., I had seen red-faced policemen drag stunned old men from their rest in ten-cent toilet stalls and press them against the yellow-cream brick of the downstairs men's room—and then roust them out into the cold night. All that was left of these lost souls were folded bits of papers and scraps of memory tossed from wallets onto the cement floor as the cops sought their identities. I had a ticket. I wasn't loitering; I was waiting.

And sleep is no easy matter in the bright-glare mumble of the terminal. The utilitarian design of the benches with their jutting armrests made it impossible to stretch out upon them. God knows the city wouldn't want to give a soul too much comfort. I ended up hooking the toe of my right foot through the left armrest and cupping my chin in the palm of my right hand with my right elbow leaning painfully and precariously on the right armrest. I slept very little though I spent the whole five hours earnestly trying. As one side of my body became numb or tingly, I would alternate toes and elbows and try again. The graying clock, which hung across from me over the ticket counter on a pastel wall, said little that was good that night.

Invisibly the world of sunshine surrounded me and slowly awareness of consciousness came to me as the northbound motion of the Greyhound gently stirred my body. I had slept deeply for a couple of hours and to me the sky was suddenly full of morning. To awake publicly is initially a time of self-consciousness so the first thing that I did was to sheepishly look around the bus—the vain nudity of sleep.

My precious blue-canvas gym bag was the next thing I thought of and I quickly felt it on the floor beneath my feet—the mountains! Where were the mountains?

Out the window to my left stretched the same flat vastness that had dominated the days before but, beyond the haze of blue, on the horizon, topped with white cloud-puffs of snow, sat the magnificence of the Rocky Mountains,

I stared incessantly westward. The mountains drifted slowly closer.

I'd come so far to arrive at that brilliant morning.

Cheyenne was an early-morning railroad and cow town. The steep angle of the sun cast long dark shadows through the maze of fences and ramps making up the railyard that dominated the south edge of town. There was little motion or sound stirring the streets.

Man, did I feel great. The all-blue sky and the cool morning Wyoming air and I was free—free from going to or coming from any place or time, and free from the chains of weariness predominant through the previous night. Free, and each step I took westward on the road was mortally fresh. I was *there* and it was absolutely real.

The late-May day was warm and the sun, almost directly overhead, intensified the dryness of the land. I was on the edge of Medicine Bow, a town which consisted of a line of faded buildings separated from the highway by a wide margin of gravel. The world stretched forever in all directions broken only by a distant snow-covered mountain range and the infinite regularity of power poles that followed the westward flow of the railroad track running parallel to the highway.

The road was almost empty. There was dust and gusting wind and harsh sun. My God, was it beautiful.

Then, out there along westbound U.S. 30, in an instant, the wind ceased and stillness exploded my soul.

It was as if, in this sudden vacuum of silence, the world-encompassing expanse had stretched so wide it released the full dimension of myself—a *self* that I could not see or explain but only *be*.

I knew a part of that moment would be with me as long as I lived.

Once one's spirit expands to the horizons, it will never truly fit the prison of petty flesh again.

A child-man's glimpse of forever. That's what it was there along the road west of Medicine Bow.

From the Infinite to California

Returning to the roadside from Forever, I caught a ride with an amazing man in a brand-new sports car.

He said, "I jump from the skies and dive to the depths of oceans and ski down and snowshoe up God's mountains and trek jungles, deserts, and all manner of terrain. My training has taken me all over the world and there is no place, no topography, and no climate that can deter me."

Cynically, I thought of "neither snow nor rain, nor…" what a hell of a mailman he could be.

Looking around at Wyoming's warming afternoon and feeling the blast of his air conditioning, I thought of how insulated life could be. Just another yarn spinner—okay, it was a real day, it was a real ride and Earth rolled beneath us.

I thought of how my voice might seem to others when I returned home and told the outlandish tales of my travels, and realized that the man wasn't nuts. He was proud and soon I was proud to know him. He was in the Air Force and especially trained to rescue astronauts and, thus, he had to master the challenges of the whole world. The spinning days of our planet were just specks of local time and who could really know where to expect the arrival of a space traveler returning from the cosmos?

He had been traveling alone for a long time, and, actually, I realized, so had I.

We talked and laughed and impressed each other and he was going to Oregon to see his ex-wife and his children. He told me a story—a tale he had read on a restaurant placemat.

There was, in western Wyoming, a sheep herder who, caught in the vastness of a Wyoming blizzard felt the certainty of his death. Blinded by the rage of winds and snow, stumbling and wrenching the reaches of his being, desperate and lost, he came upon the shelter of an abandoned shack and survived because of it. Thus, dedicated by the gift of life, he swore on the spot of his salvation that no passing creature would find desolation. That, according to the legend, was the inspiration for the mecca known as Little

America. Little America, I realized as we pulled into the parking lot, was a multiplicity of motels, gas stations, and restaurants owned by a keeper of the sheep or at least a puller of the wool.

Whether the story was true or not, the food that my benefactor provided for me there was tremendous. I ate, at his insistence (though he didn't need to prod much) a vast amount of beef and bread and potatoes and felt that whatever the days of the future held for me, I would never have need of more food.

Little America is where highway U.S. 30 North separates from Highway 30 South. U.S. 30 North streams directly toward Oregon, while 30 South takes a dip through Utah and Salt Lake City before it rejoins the direction of its northern brother. Originally my friend had intended to take the northern, more direct route but for my behalf he extended my ride with him by swinging south.

Again, I felt the effect of receiving a genuine gift.

Thumbing on south through Utah and across the tip of Nevada, and through Las Vegas and into California...

Yes! *California!*

Man was I in the West.

The best ride was a good long hitch with a laconic cowboy-booted and high-hatted and "yep" and "nope" speaking fellow in a pickup truck. He earned his pay as a mail sorter in a Salt Lake post office. A misplaced man who worked his nights pressing occasional buttons in an automated factory and reading books. He was taking a three-day foray out upon the road. I wondered if he and I were all that much different.

Welcome to California: the Desert and the Nudist Guru

Los Angeles was a crazy human blur.

I was warned, though. Three hours before I made my triumphant arrival in the mythic city I had been warned. "You don't want to go down into that mess, stay up here on the mountain with me." This was a prophetic pronouncement of the sixty-year-old-man who had picked me up in his red Alpha Romeo and who had taken the back way to San Bernardino across the mountain via an old dirt road.

He parked the car and said that we would climb up the slope.

"We'll leave our shirts here in the car."

He climbed up the steep slope ahead of me with amazing agility.

"You'd have a nice body if you'd stand up straight," he called down to me as I heaved my way up.

I staggered to a small level place and he showed me how to drink water from a spring-filled puddle without stirring up the mud bottom. His was one well-tanned old man.

"I've got a wife and two kids. I've given them all that a man can afford to give and they're pretty well burnt out on me, too. A couple of years ago, I fixed my room up out on the sun porch and I've slept out there ever since.

He climbed higher up the ridge of the mountain following a path made by passing deer.

Either the trail was less steep or I was becoming accustomed to it. I wasn't breathing as hard and found it was easier to keep up with him. He seemed to be studying me.

The conversations we had were of ideas and purposes and directions, and he listened hard to my answers to his questions.

We came to a place where a large rock jutted out above the trees and we climbed out to the tip of it. Before us stretched the desert spreading far to the east. Little was said for a while and then he began to speak.

He told me that I was nineteen years old (a fact that bartenders and beer salesmen across the country had not been able to discern) and that I had been with few women if any, and that the things I was seeking in mountains and oceans could not be found in superficial dabbling but required a more meaningful, deeper, more natural form of communication. Communication between myself in my most natural state and the pure eternal soul of nature.

"When my transparent wife and sterile kids push me beyond a point, I drive up here on the mountain or out there on the desert and throw off my clothes and walk silently, reverently into nature. Nudity frees me. Nudity frees me of the threads with which civilization binds a man. Clothes are encumbrances that make a man a loud and clumsy visitor to nature rather than a participant in it."

The man was speaking to me and though I was totally aware of what he was saying, another portion of my mind was recording disbelief of the fact that I was sitting on the side of a mountain three-thousand miles from home with a nudist.

"Look, I'm no threat to you. This is not a sexual matter with me. Why don't I go back on down the mountain and you walk over into those trees and try it?"

An evangelical nudist at that!

"I don't want to force you into this by any means and I'll assure you it's not my intention to sneak behind the trees and stare at you or steal your pants. (Jeez, I hadn't thought of him stealing my pants.)

There was nothing perverted about this man or the thing that he wanted me to do. But for me to drop drawers and skinny into the woods at this moment would have been quite perverted.

"Don't let me force you now but why don't you try it? It's the most liberating feeling in the world."

"Well, I don't think I'd be very good at this at first and what if I step over a limb that's a little higher than I'd anticipated?"

"Clothes smother and dull the parts of your body, the moment that you become nude out here you will become totally aware of your whole body. I can wander through these trees and not disturb a leaf or a twig and stand just a few feet from wild animals that no longer fear me."

"Oh... well, I don't think that I want to try it today." My voice was hesitant. I didn't want to offend the man but I didn't want to take my clothes off either. My mind, searching logical excuses landed on nudist jokes and I said, "I'd sure hate to get a sunburn."

"Nonsense," he smiled, "I'll say no more about it but do remember what I've told you and whenever the time is right for you, free yourself."

We walked back down the slope talking of lighter things like death and war. It was when we got back to the car that he warned me about Los Angeles. He told me there were other things that he could tell me but respected that I had to travel on. So, I was back on the highway at San Bernardino watching him drive away and knowing that meeting him was a good thing.

Strange, yes. But good.

(And years later, I finally got around to buffing it in in the wilds. He was right.)

Rest and Redetermination in Glendale

My little red-headed aunt, a couple of years senior to my little red-headed mother, was afraid I had died.

A ride had swept me down the valley and left me in the cluttered and somewhat dangerous heart of downtown Los Angeles. It was street-people and drugger alleys. At least that's the way it seemed to me, a lad from safer haven. What ever happened to the "City of Angels" my mother told me about?

In 1934 at the age of twenty-six, my mother took a transcontinental Greyhound Bus trip from Roanoke, Virginia, out to visit her sister, Blandine (my Aunt Billie), who lived in Glendale, California. The version of California Mom told me about as a kid was aglow with her blue-eyed wonder. It was a paradise of natural and cultural marvels, and, wow, was it a great place to party. She and Aunt Billie and Uncle Verd and an impressive parade of her suitors managed to dance away many a great night during the months of Mom's visit. A few years ago, over twenty years beyond her passing at 79, I discovered a four-page single-spaced treasure that has enriched my whole concept of who my mother was. It is the journal of that fantastic trip—a free-flowing stream of adventure and discovery and, mostly fun, that tells the odyssey of an Eastern-Kentucky-born (Ball Fork/Scant Branch/Pinson Fork/Pike County) child of an emerging century; a flapper, a teen bride/mother/divorcee, a bindery worker/proofreader, true believer in joy, naïve and knowing journeyer to the promised land of Los Angeles before the La-Las took over.

Yeah, that was my mama—little did we know of the sweet lady who sang my sister Nancy and I awake in the morning and met us at the door with after-school cookies. I've written that my father is my strength and my mother my poetry. Well, it turns out, my mom might also be the wildness that drives me as well.

I'll include her whole travel-and-celebration journal in an appendix. Please take time to read it—she might also be the source of the writer I have strived to be.

So, there I was, road-weary, wary, and thoroughly disillusioned. Drunks on the sidewalks dangerous-looking crazy people darting about, sad losers of the game of life—what happened to Mama's California?

I thought, "I've got to get out of here." Instead of hanging around absorbing the dire poetry of the streets, I hopped a northbound city bus bound for Glendale and my little red-headed Aunt Billie.

She wasn't surprised when I showed up on her doorstep. I guess Mom had told her I might be wandering in sometime that early summer. It wasn't really so much who I was when I said, "Hello, Aunt Billie." It was what must have looked like. The last time I had really had a good look into a mirror, I had been a nineteen-year-old kid combing his hair in the upstairs bathroom of my parent's house. In the weeks ensuing I had become a creature of the road. Though I had kept up the basics of personal hygiene at stops along the way and in gas station bathrooms—a bit of a shave here, a scrub there, and somewhere in my gym bag I occasionally found my hairbrush. I wasn't some unkempt hobo lad just rambling in from the rails.

But… I wasn't the kid who had packed up and hit the road a few weeks earlier. I think it was mainly the eyes. Something alert, wary, even hardened. It took her a moment, but my Aunt Billie didn't fluster easily. "Bobby Lee, look at you."

I had no idea how tired I was. I hadn't really slept for several days. It seemed one ride just led to another and when it got dark, the guys who picked me up, two nights in a row, had asked me to drive while they slept. On the long run into L.A., I had driven a great big pickup truck. I got a kick out of it, but the hours were bearing down pretty hard on me when I finished a wonderful sandwich and some fruit and juice. I took a good long shower and put on a robe she had found for me while she washed my clothes. Looking around her beautiful little yellow house with its books and knick-knacks and out the window at the lemon tree, I got a touch of the magic my mother had described as California.

"Are those real lemons on that tree, Aunt Billie?"

… and then I went to sleep.

I mean really to sleep.

I think it came out to something like sixteen hours—from late afternoon until around nine the next morning when I awoke to find my aunt sitting in a straight-backed chair in the corner of the sleeping porch where I was bedded.

I said good morning to her and she smiled and said, "Well, good morning to you, Bobby Lee. I thought you might be dead."

I spent most of a great week with Aunt Billie and Uncle Charlie (a fine fellow—Aunt Billie's fourth and final husband). I had never before nor have I since ingested such an array of healthy foods: fresh fruits, juices, green stuff. She took me on grand tours of places like Forest Lawn Cemetery and Mt. Wilson Observatory. What fun.

I visited for a couple days with cousins in El Monte. Everyone was really nice to me. The lure of comfort and good people—I could really have gotten used to Southern California living. But I knew then, as I do now, *I was born to wander.*

It wasn't the California paradise of my mother that I sought; it was the San Francisco of Kerouac.

Late in the afternoon the day before I was to leave, she and I drove out to Santa Monica where Highway 66 terminates at the Pacific. I swear, my sixty-something-year-old aunt consistently ran the freeways at a good ten miles an hour over her age. Wherever we went, it was a thrill.

The sun was nearly setting when we walked out to the overlook and it all came together there. I had never seen anything like that sunset. I couldn't even speak. It was then that Aunt Billie just kind of put it all into perspective for me: who I was, where I was, and where I had come from. She said, "When your mama came out here on a Greyhound bus on her trip in the thirties, I brought her to right where you and I are standing today. And it was another marvelous sunset—like now. And, it was just so beautiful that she broke down and cried... it was so beautiful to her."

Yes.

California Bleeding

It was such a miserable gray day. The rain was steady. I sat on a large rock watching the ocean and watching my knee bleed through the rip in my pants. The ocean was dark and terrible—it was so powerful and I felt so weak, so small.

The whole thing started way back in Kansas when I stopped at my uncle's house just outside of Topeka. We drank a few beers and started talking about the motorcycle sitting in his next-door neighbor's driveway—why those things don't use any gasoline at all, you could drive all day on almost nothing—I could really make some time on one of those things, and I wouldn't have to stay on the main roads. If I saw an old lonely road cutting out toward some big mountain, I could just get on that road and see where it goes. I could buy myself a couple of blankets and sleep under the trees—yes, instead of my head twisted back over some stranger's front seat. But, my uncle said, just be sure that you don't have yourself a flat tire—amen, that'd be an ugly way to go... but I'd be careful and besides, one of those strangers might break my head and dump me into some river. Yeah, Uncle Junior planted the idea. "Bobby, that would sure be a good way to travel."

And then, on the long ride I caught from Santa Barbara on the way from Aunt Billie's up to San Francisco, I talked with a fellow who had driven a Harley Davidson all the way from Philadelphia to the coast—and claimed it was the best thing he'd ever done. This fellow had the second most unusual occupation that I had encountered in my travels. The first prize went to the traveling prophylactic salesman in Kansas. This man was a fire engine salesman and naturally enough had done a tremendous amount of traveling. It was during a discussion of all the places he had been that we got on to the subject of motorcycles and his trip across the country.

I had come to California for an ocean and now I was rolling north on U.S. 101 and knew that just a few miles west of this major highway there was State Highway 1 twisting and riding the blue-lapping edge of the country. And I had come to California to be free and now I was locked into a stream of travel rather than experience. No, I hadn't been to Winnemucca, Nevada

You can see how this is heading for a motorcycle, a rainy desperate day, and a bloody knee.

It was almost dark when we got to San Francisco. It wasn't until I watched him drive off that I noticed how red his car was.

A Night at the Ritz

San Francisco.

I wandered around for about a half hour trying to get up enough nerve to go into one of the cheap hotels and get a room.   There was something about the thin-faced old men who inhabited the ancient lobbies of the dollar-and-a–half a night places that scared me away.   I bought an orange.   Darkness was very near now and I knew I'd have to settle somewhere.   It was strange how through all the dark empty nights with eerie winds, and the night-scene threat of cities across the country, and the crazy people who had picked me up—all of these things and now it was the staring of old men in old hotels that frightened me.

I finally found the Ritz Hotel.   It was two dollars a night but the lobby was empty.

I decided to get drunk.   I wandered around the steep hills and listened to the night sounds of the harbor.   I was looking for a liquor store that had the appearance of one that would be willing to sell a nineteen-year-old kid a bottle of wine.   There was something about the size of the city and all of the people around me that made me feel like a kid for the first time since I'd left home, and if you don't have confidence when you go into a liquor store your chances of getting served are pretty bad.   Cities always had a way of making me enjoy being absolutely invisible.   Nobody giving a damn about anyone else had always been a great source of insulation.   Cities leave a kid alone and when you're a kid, that really feels good sometimes.

But things were different.   I had known my soul's explosion on the desert.   I had seen myself impossibly large and real, and now I was very small and invisible.   "Shit!   Nobody's going to sell a boy a bottle of wine."

"That'll be seventy-nine cents, Sir, thank you.   Come again."

A man in a new town walking down the street with a bottle of wine in a bag gripped by his left hand. It wasn't too long after I'd bought the wine that it occurred to me that there wasn't any place for me to go to drink my bottle except back at the hotel.   The room was small and pale. The bed looked like one you might find in a Southern mental institution for the poor. It was a rack of metal with a thin mattress, but it was a place to sit and drink my Chianti and think about how cool I was to be in San Francisco drinking a bottle of wine. I felt like one of Jack Kerouac's *Dharma Bums.*

About halfway through, the bottle the alcohol started working on me. I interrupted a serious attempt to write a poem with rolling around on the mattress laughing and kicking about how the week I had spent down in Glendale with my Aunt Billie and her pure fruit juices had turned me into a wino. Everything was funny then. I opened the shade and looked out my window and into a window of the cheap hotel across the alley from the Ritz. I started thinking about naked women and how cheap hotels were famous for cheap naked women. I opened the door of the room and looked up and down the purple-carpeted hall—just in case there was a naked woman out there waiting for me. There wasn't.

I finished the bottle and decided that I was ready for the streets. (Look out you San Francisco. Look out you wild city, here I come.) I lumbered down the stairs and out into the night. The air was surprisingly cool. My mind was not lost; it was simply disjointed from reality—I thought I could handle anything the city had.

I was walking down a dark cross street which connected two brightly lit streets. The man who walked toward me was well dressed and dignified looking.

"I'm kind of wild, how about you?"

"No man, I'm not that kind of wild."

"Sure."

I walked on but when I looked back somehow out of the shadows of doorways three other men had appeared. I walked faster and saw that they were getting closer to me. It was then that I started running for the bright lights a half block ahead of me. I didn't know whether they were a marauding group of thugs or a group of marauders out after thugs—but I was certain that for the moment I was their prey. I could hear their footsteps echoing in the narrow street. They were getting closer.

(Help! You see there's this boy in California who doesn't know anybody and he's being chased by a bunch of fiends.)

There was a bright doorway ahead of me (my God, it's an all-night grocery store). I ran through the door and hid behind a mountainous display of New Blue Cheer. I never saw my pursuers again—I suppose that they simply went back to their black doorways to wait.

The bright lights led back to the Ritz and I spent the rest of the night there—sleeping and listening to the next-door toilet flushing.

Letter to Carol from the Ritz Hotel

Notice the difference in tone and content between the previous chapter and the following letter. It reminds me of a letter I discovered while going through my father's papers after he died. It was from his brother, my Uncle Charles, written from the battlefront at Anzio, Italy, during WWII. Uncle Charles just wrote about missing home and, "How are you doing, Bob," and, "Well, I've got to get back to work." Nothing of the horrors of that struggle.

Carol,

I'm in a small cheap hotel (the Ritz) in San Francisco. I love you—It's a good city up and down, fog, cable cars, Chinamen, the whole bit and it's real too. I've been walking around for a few hours and my legs are weak from the hills (cliffs). I love you. I bought a bottle of Chianti wine for 79 cents and plan on taking it easy the rest of the evening—I saw the big ships in the harbor and heard the deep fog horns—the fog makes things eerie and chilly—I wonder who's been in this bed before me? Los Angeles is for crap. What I saw of Southern California proved to be a great disappointment—It doesn't rain there so there isn't any water—where they don't constantly irrigate there is desert and the valleys are full of smog and white powdery dust from factories and more cars than I've ever seen, and bigger trucks and no gentle rivers only concrete ones with only dry white dust and no water—the money is in real estate and the sky scrapers are banks, savings and loans, and insurance companies—the people outwardly impress much like Miami, Florida, people—a little gaudy. The ocean and the mountains were all I wanted or expected them to be but it's only on the exceptional windy days you can see the mountains through the smog and only on the mid-week or cold days you can feel the beach for the noisy crowds of people—and the modern, beautiful buildings are so new that the shrubs and trees are small and the grass is dry sod. But up through the valleys north it gets gradually better and better—then you come to thousands of trees in straight, handsome, cultivated, irrigated rows and each tree is heavy with hundreds of bright beautiful oranges and you feel like you can breathe again just from seeing them.   Further north and the orchards disappear and a quilt-work of shades of green crops spreads flat out to the base of steep dark hills and mountains.   When Frisco was close I saw heavy low clouds and asked with sadness, "Smog?" and the man laughed and said "No, *Fog!*"   It's all here, Carol—but wait… a verse—

The city, the sounds,
the harbor, the sea,
my bed and my bottle
and I but need thee.

And a pun—The boy is beautiful but without you I feel more like a buoy than a man.   Or a song—"I left my heart in Cape Girardeau."   Or a dance—Tap Tap Tap Tap Tap Tap Tap (translation: I love you).   When I see you next, remind me to croon you the Carol Riehl song I sang for you in San Francisco.

It's real late or real early—however you think of it—so I took a walk—the streets were full of pimps and drag queens.   (Therefore, fulfilling the big city promise of prostitutes and substitutes.)

May, 1964

I don't know that I ever mailed this letter.   I think the wine got to me before I finished and I just went to sleep.

The Motorcycle: the Cost of Freedom

When I was in Los Angeles my aunt cashed a check for me so I had plenty of money. I went down to the Greyhound Bus Terminal and bought a ticket to Petaluma which is about forty miles north of San Francisco. The bus ride would leave me clear of the city where rides would be easier to get.

Petaluma had a long street of glass windows and I went into the door of a window full of motorcycles. (FREEDOM. Nobody's going to hold me back.) I could buy a motorcycle—railroad money had been good, I had a bank-full of the damned stuff.

"It'll go seventy miles an hour, get one hundred and twenty-five miles per gallon, and besides, with this flashy helmet all the women are going to love you."

"How much?"

"Look, man. It's only two years old and it's been treated like royalty."

"Was she a little-old-lady school teacher?"

"$350.00."

"Ok."

It took a day to get the money wired to me. I just went to a $1.50 hotel and slept. I went to a surplus store and almost bought a blanket. All I really wanted to do was get out of Petaluma.

"By the way. Do you know how to drive a motorcycle?"

"Hell no! I've never been on a motorcycle."

Four forwards and 150cc.

"Oh well, I'll drive you around the block a couple of times. You'll figure it out."

(Freedom here I come.)

I Didn't Buy the Flashy Helmet

I didn't buy the flashy helmet but I did buy a dollar pair of goggles and some elastic straps to hold my blue gym bag onto the back of the bike.

And so it was—the happy seeker four-speeding it up the highway at a big 55 mph—not quite seventy but nobody was holding me back. The blue sky said, "Roll on, man. You've got the world and 125 miles per gallon.'

There are twisting mountain roads in northern California and when your little Japanese motor sputters you are really alone.

I tried to ignore the fact that my $350 motorcycle had sputtered but it did it again and then quit completely. I coasted to the bottom of the hill and thought, "Spark plug."

I don't know why—it was likely the only possibility I thought I could fix.

The strange thing was that for a moment I didn't know what to do. I had owned my own transportation for maybe four hours and already I had forgotten how to get from one place to another. I had been so damned free that the stalling of an engine had left me momentarily helpless.

I heard the sound of an approaching car and began hitchhiking for help.

Leggett, California, had less than five hundred people but still supported a motorcycle store. I walked toward the store and noticed a county police car pull into the parking lot. I went up to the store and said, "Spark plug."

About a half an hour later the policeman and I were staring at my useless motorcycle.

"Son, you don't need a spark plug—you're just out of gas."

"But I haven't gone any 250 miles on my two gallons of gas."

"Just turn this lever and your reserve tank will get you to a filling station."

I thanked the policeman for his help and for the ride and climbed aboard my freedom ship and headed toward the next town. I had gotten gas once that day but had stopped because of the bathroom—not suspecting that I needed gas (seventy cents is a lot of gasoline for a two-gallon tank).

And in a $2 hotel that night I knew that my money couldn't buy me the distance home or even the distance to my nearest check-cashing friend or relative. And it troubled me that I didn't have enough money. Not so much that I didn't sleep though—I was exhausted.

It was sometime late that next gray rainy morning that, as I was pulling into the gravel parking lot of a roadside tavern, both of my precious two wheels slid out from under me and flattened me to the ground.

I just lay there for a while.

I wasn't killed but my leg hurt and, when I found that the bike would still run, I took off up the highway until I came to a deserted beach.

I parked my not-so-shiny black motorcycle by the road and limped out to the lonely rock facing the terrible gray sea and thought about freedom.

And thus was that I came to that miserable day south of Crescent City with an aching knee and a daunted spirit.

Bob and Alvin Lackey

Another night in a cheap hotel. Crescent City, California. June, 1964.

I woke up tired. Yeah, tired and stiff and my knee hurt and my clothes were still damp. And, oh yes. I was nearly out of cash and a solid 3000 miles from home.

I limped down the long stairway to the sidewalk and as I stepped out into the chill of a worrisome new day—surprise! It was raining.

I realized I was about half afraid of the damned little Honda 150 motorcycle parked out on the curb. The thing had hurt me. I strapped my gym bag to the back fender, turned on the key and kick-started it to life. The nifty electric start button had been ruined in the wreck.

I'm not going to tell you all these sorry details just to get your sympathy. I want you to know just how discouraged and miserable I felt so you might appreciate the full impact of Bob and Alvin Lackey on my worldview then and still, over fifty years later.

The road can make you bitter. It's the raw edges of harsh weather and stark loneliness. The fatigue, the toil of unceasing distances. The false promise of the next turn taken, the next hill crested—the dismal truth of futures realized. It can break down your spirit and your flesh and you're still a long way from home.

That's the way it was for nineteen-year-old Robert that morning leaving Crescent City, California, with a bum knee and a damaged motorcycle: a rainy highway and a continent to cross. I was through with the coast and its gray sea, its slashing storms and its treacherous gravel parking lots.

And it wasn't just the ache of a road-chafed body and the chill of the weather. That bastard motorcycle salesman had lied to me. 125 miles per gallon, my ass.

I guess, mainly, I just felt foolish.

Yeah, I needed to cut the dream short and head back east. With the little money I had I would get as far as the buzzing little bike would go. Gas was cheap back then, maybe forty cents a gallon. I figured, roughly, it was a little under a penny a mile and, if I didn't eat or sleep in a hotel or waste a dime on any other such creature comforts, I had just enough cash to maybe make it the 1900 miles to Topeka, Kansas, where my Uncle Junior was stationed at Forbes Air Force Base. He would cash a check for me and I could get home.

You see, that was the morning when my travel ceased to be an adventure and became a task.

So, with a twenty-dollar bill in my wallet and a few crumpled ones crammed in my jeans, I pulled out on to Highway 101 northbound and then took 199, the slant road to the northeast—and began a treacherous, life-changing sixty-mile journey to Cave Junction, Oregon.

Whatever the wreck and the crooked salesman hadn't wrenched out of my self-confidence, Highway 199 just about finished off.

Yes, I'd better tell you about Bob and Alvin Lackey. They saved me in 1964. Maybe in the political and social turmoil of 2017, they will again.

U.S. 199

How many of us can recall the exact day when we realized that on a gut-deep, visceral level, we are not immortal? Are we less naïve once we realize that we are naïve? Is the world a safer place for us when we deeply acknowledge our frail mortality?

When we sense how truly small we are, does it become easier for us to hide?

June, 1964. Cold, damp, bruised, nearly broke and a continent away from home. Yeah, that was a rough morning when I buzzed my little Honda motorcycle north out of Crescent City, California. But, hell, rough days were just part of the grand experience, right?

Sometimes it's like a gathering storm, the elements assembled and massing upon moments that so harshly portend our collapse.

U.S. Highway 199 makes an eighty-mile long run from the coast north of Crescent City diagonally northeast up through Cave Junction, Oregon, and ends at Grants Pass. That morning I had studied my road maps seeking the most direct route from Northern California to Topeka, Kansas and my Uncle Junior. This seemed the road to take.

Just a few details and then some thoughts.

You've heard the sound of a huge truck coming down a mountain with its Jake Brake on. Its real name is the Jacobs Compression Brake—a valve that uses engine compression to slow the vehicle and save the air brakes from overheating and become useless. It's a loud *rat-a-daddle, daddle* sound so abrasive that many mountain communities have ordinances with stiff fines prohibiting its use.

The biggest trees in the world are redwoods. They are a marvel to experience. Meditate for a moment in a grove of these massive pillars and it changes your perspective of the whole world. In the right frame of mind, you feel as if you are surrounded by gentle, cloud-shrouded giants. In the wrong frame, you'll just feel small— like bug small.

Highway 199 for many miles is a ledge carved into the stone cliffs overlooking the twisting, whitewater rush of the Smith River. The edge of the road is often the brink of a precipice dropping sharply down to the swirling stream. It is a truly harrowing drive.

Let us gather the factors together and add to the mix my recently acquired fear of wet-road curves. And, the rain. Let's not forget the rain.

Okay. Now picture Bobby Lee Nichols, a nineteen-year-old with maybe two full days' worth of experience on his tiny, 150cc Honda motorcycle. Two days, one slick-road crash, and 3000 miles to go.

I had to go slow, otherwise I was certain I would just slide right off and into the abyss at every one the interminable succession of serpentine switchbacks. So, of course, the massive logging trucks hovering inches behind my flickering little taillight were constantly, *rat-a-daddle-daddle,* Jake-Braking and scaring the shorts off of me—I could feel the breath of their raging diesel engines bearing down on me like roaring, ravenous, fire-breathing dragons. And at every widening of the canyon those huge trees, freakish in their dimension, just crushed me with their unnatural mass.

This highway with its breathtaking scenic intensity, the redwoods with their soul-soaring immensity—the raw exhilaration of interaction of road, nature and consciousness—became one of my favorites of all the roads of this nation. But such was the context of that dismal, frightening first encounter, that I only knew it as a venue of mortal terror.

Yes, it was probably on the fifteenth consecutive hair-raising turn with blinding deluge of mist and rain, vicious roar of logging trucks, rock-slide rubble treacherously scattered upon the slippery pavement, and the raging torrent of the ever-deadly river just beyond the narrow strip of asphalt upon which I so tenuously rode that the thought, for the first time in my young life, occurred to me: Oh, my God! I might not make it.

Let's see. Over fifty years ago. I haven't been the same since.

Interestingly, it hadn't been the carload of murderous pigs, the big-city cop who drove me out of a midnight ghetto neighborhood with "Hell, kid, you could have been killed just standing there by the road." It hadn't been the risk of thumbing down rides from strangers clear across the country. No, my mortal reckoning came not so much from obvious physical threat as from a core-deep sense of discouragement.

I recall pulling onto a "slow traffic pull-off" lane and letting the parade of monster trucks and impatient Californians pass and thinking, "What the hell am I doing here?"

I mean, the country I was travelling though was the epitome of the West that I had sought in the journey. Incredibly lush, and powerful vistas of mountains and streams and the richness of weather upon my sentient flesh. Yes!

But, given the cocktail of insecurity I had ingested over the previous two days—the daunting truths of exposure, vulnerability and, especially, economics—instead of being exhilarated and inspired, I was only damp and scared.

I emerged from the canyon and rode into the widening Illinois River Valley with no sense of accomplishment. The threat was lessened, but the wound to my confidence was fresh. It was just a good thing that I had been taught that men don't cry.

The lying motorcycle salesman back in Petaluma told me to be sure to check the oil regularly. I pulled to the side of the road and stiffly dismounted. Sure enough, the damned bike was an oil burner. It was a quarter-inch down from the minimum level line. Okay. Maybe that was the one honest thing he had uttered. Actually, I'm more aggravated about the deal now, more than fifty years later, than I was back then. On that drizzling day, I was too distracted by my misery to bother adding gullibility to the list of humiliating sources of self-deprecation. I felt wet, clumsy, and hopeless. Why bother adding stupid to the list?

Years later I wrote a song about my wonderful dog, Rainbow, who was rescued by my wife Carol and my daughter Kristin from abandonment—storm-soaked along a mountain road.

One verse says:

Now Rainbow's sleeping by a fire—
he's dry and warm and safe from life's abuse.
Only hours have passed since his great trauma—
there's hope for road-lost creatures on the loose.

… road-lost creatures on the loose.

That's what I was that day and, bless me, there was hope for me. It was a damned good thing for me that Bob and Alvin Lackey were sitting around a potbelly wood stove at their Sinclair gas station at Cave Junction. I don't know what kind of a cowering wimp of lily-livered flesh I might have become if it weren't for the heartening encounter I had with these compassionate gentlemen.

I pulled into a Sinclair station to buy oil. The name over the door was "Bob and Alvin Lackey".

I walked on in.

A hint of the scent of wood smoke, wafting waves of gentle heat: Haven.

Bob and Alvin weren't big talkers. One of them said I should sit down with them and warm up a bit. It was the second time I had felt like crying that day—but, this time it was for joy.

I told them I needed oil for my motorcycle. "Okay. You just stay by the stove. I'll take care of it."

I didn't need any encouragement to stay by that miracle of warmth and security. The truth was, I had immediately determined to sit by that potbelly altar for the rest of my life.

So, maybe it was Bob who asked, "Where you heading, boy?"

"Virginia," I said and it truly sounded ridiculous.

"Hmmm," he responded.

Maybe it was Alvin who came back in and took off his yellow slicker and hung it on a hook by the door. "It took a half pint. Keep an eye on it. Don't let that little motor run dry."

"Yes, sir," I said.

I knew I had to leave. It was almost noon and I had such a long way to go. Yeah, I needed to tear myself from safety and head on back out into the elements. But, you know, it wasn't the same. I didn't have that queasy pang of fear undercutting my will. It was going to be rough, but, by God, there was "hope for road-lost creatures on the loose."

And here it is: the part of this story where humanity surpasses the impersonal wrath of nature.

One of those guardian-angel Lackey brothers put a hand on my shoulder as I walked to door and with the other hand grabbed his yellow-slicker raincoat from the hook. "Here, boy. You wear this."

And the other brother rose from his seat and came over. He shook my hand and forced a five-dollar bill into my palm. "You take care now. And don't worry about the oil, we'll give it to you."

I don't really know what words of gratitude I uttered. I know they were insufficient to express the depth of appreciation I felt. I did tell them I would pay them back someday. They just shook their heads and smiled.

I kicked the engine to a revv'ng hum, dropped the pedal into gear and left.

Some years later, educated, married and driving down the west coast in a decent car with Carol, I pulled into the Cave Junction filling station, walked in, and found Bob and Alvin by the stove right where I had encountered them the first time. I didn't want to embarrass them so I just thanked them one last time, gave them five dollars and said, "And, if you don't mind, I think I'll just keep the raincoat."

We three laughed for a moment, nodded farewell, and that was it.

I know those good men are long gone by now. I wish they could read what I have finally gotten around to writing all these years too late.

I said the frightening realization of my own mortal vulnerability that despairing day in the terrible canyon changed my life. Well, let me tell you, sure I am less careless in my adventures, but also, for all these decades of succeeding days, I have been changed by the gifts of Bob and Alvin Lackey. My metaphorical glass is almost always at least half full.

Rescue

The curse of the damned motorcycle was not yet dispelled.

Somewhere east of Grants Pass on the highway that traverses the southern lands of Oregon, I was roaring (well, actually, whirring) down a long straight grade approaching the promised 70 mph the salesman had assured me. My goggles cleared for a moment and I realized that the road came to a "T" just ahead. I knew in the dampness if I rammed on the brakes I would be spread all over the asphalt. I saw on the cross road a couple of Oregon's ubiquitous logging trucks, a scatter of high-speed cars and a flash of a gap between. Still maintaining most of my 70 mph, I shot for the gap, lunged across the highway and blasted out into an open field on the other side. No barbed-wire fence. No forest. No raging stream. Pure luck. It was just nice hay. I didn't even crash.

But, by time I got the bike turned around and back to the edge of the road, I had determined that, at any price, I was going to sell that miserable machine as soon as possible.

Klamath Falls had a Honda dealership.

$125 was a lot of money to lose in 1964. Even at the good wage paid at the railroad yard, it was over a week's labor. The salesman had looked over the scratches and the busted starter button and offered me $225 for my $350 motorcycle.

I didn't hesitate. "Sure," I said. And when he told me he couldn't pay me until he got a title from California—probably a couple of months. Hey, I didn't care. "Sure," I said. "Mail me a check."

And then as I walked out of that store with some kind of paperwork stuffed into my gym bag, I almost whooped.

Damn, I was glad to get away from that machine and afoot out upon the street where my course of travel was at the whim of a capricious destiny. I really felt free.

The ordeal wasn't over though.

Klamath Falls, back in those days, was not the friendliest town in the West—at least it didn't seem so to me. I left the Honda store and went into a gas station restroom and cleaned up. I shaved and shined a bit—putting on my presentable roadside appearance. It was a bustling town. I strolled on through the downtown area to a wide place in the road, and stood there for hours upon hours as parading drivers cruised on past me without even a glance my way. It was late day when a pair of guys wearing cowboy hats and jewelry, maybe a touch of perfume, picked me up and told me I didn't have a chance in hell at catching a ride in that town. They took me out to the edge where there was a triangular island where the highways split and pointed me to the road vectored toward the southeast, wished me luck and with a laugh turned around and headed back into town. And…I stood there for some more hours— maybe eleven all totaled in that town. I think it still holds the record for the longest stretch of roadside thumbing I have ever endured. After successfully crossing the entire width of the United States riding the magic of that thumb, somehow in this bland little burg in the middle of nowhere I seemed to hardly exist.

Well, actually, I was not completely overlooked.

I was really fatigued when the carful of clean-cut kids pulled up about 75 feet away and got out to examine me. I, tired and somewhat stifled in my enthusiasm for the journey, just glared back at them when one of the lads took a step toward me, lifted a slingshot, pulled it back and shot me squarely in the breastbone with a marble.

Road-worn, aggravated, and really in pain, I went nuts. I charged at the bunch of goddamned thugs. Laughing, they jumped in the car and sped off. Aha, but little did these assholes know that in my Little League baseball days I was a somewhat renowned outfielder. I scooped up a nice-sized stone on the run and with a curse and a mighty hurl, I bounced the righteous rock right off their rear window. I can't swear that it broke, but one can surely hope so.

It did hurt, but I felt pretty good about the toss. I've still got a dent where the marble hit me.

I walked back to my place by the road, State Highway 140 I think it was. I couldn't believe what a lousy string of days I was having.

But, I'll tell you, journeys are not about quitting. If they were then they would be called sojourns in nowhere—lifelong layovers in narrow little towns along narrow useless highways.

And also, and this is so important, there are angels out there. I swear there are. Not some wing-and-harp cloud dwellers—no, I'm talking about the fleshy manifestations of God's love that show up when it gets to be more than you can handle by yourself. Angels like Bob and Alvin back in Cave Junction. And a whole carload of beautiful brown-faced angels who gave me safe haven—the gift of a ride on through that dark night.

A rancher in a pickup truck had pulled over and offered to take me a few miles out of town. I said, "Sure, thanks," and jumped in—anything to get out of Klamath Falls. What could be worse?

Well…how about the darkest, shadow-haunted, empty run of road in all the U.S. of A.?

"So long," he said as he turned off on a dirt lane and disappeared. I was a man of the road by then—experienced in the rigors of wind and danger and neglect, but at heart, I was still just a lad from the suburbs and more than a bit terrified by the wilds.

After a quick assessment of my predicament, the felt-black lightlessness, the shifting, crackling wind sounds of the forest, and the unlikely notion that this deep into the night there would ever be another car passing my way, I said something like, "Holy crap, there are animals out there that want to rip my head off."

Then my eyes adjusted and I saw in the slit of sky revealed through the road-course break in the trees the most glorious depth of a million stars my streetlight-occluded eyes had ever seen.

Sometimes it seems our lives are but the situations we are in. But, then there are moments of epiphany when we realize our lives are what we discover beyond the backdrop of immediate circumstance. I was beat-up weary, strained to exhaustion, hopelessly lost upon the way, and aching with a marble-sized dent in my sternum, when I perceived in the heavens an exaltation of blessing from an infinite universe.

Wow.

As long as the bears and cougars didn't get me, I knew that all the trials of the motorcycle debacle, the cold disregard of the folks of the Klamath Valley, the self-righteous meanness of the vigilante boys had brought me to the exact place upon all of God's Earth where I was supposed to be that late spring chilling night of my nineteenth year.

And then the carload of angels arrived to give me rest and comfort and a good long ride.

They may have been Native Americans or maybe Mexicans—I didn't know. I was standing pretty much in the middle of the road laughing with the stars when the old car came to a stop. The back door opened and a round woman wrapped in a blanket stepped out and said, "Come on, boy. You get in here where it's warm." Such a gentle voice, tender and yet strong and all I could say was, "Yes, ma'am."

I was cushioned between Earth Mother angels in the backseat. The driver switched on the dome light and with a broad smiling face he said over his shoulder, "We're going a long way tonight, my friend, you just relax."

And as the woman in the front seat turned and smiled at me he shut off the light and, nestled in a cloud of warmth, I settled in and we floated on into the night.

Safe or, perhaps, saved.

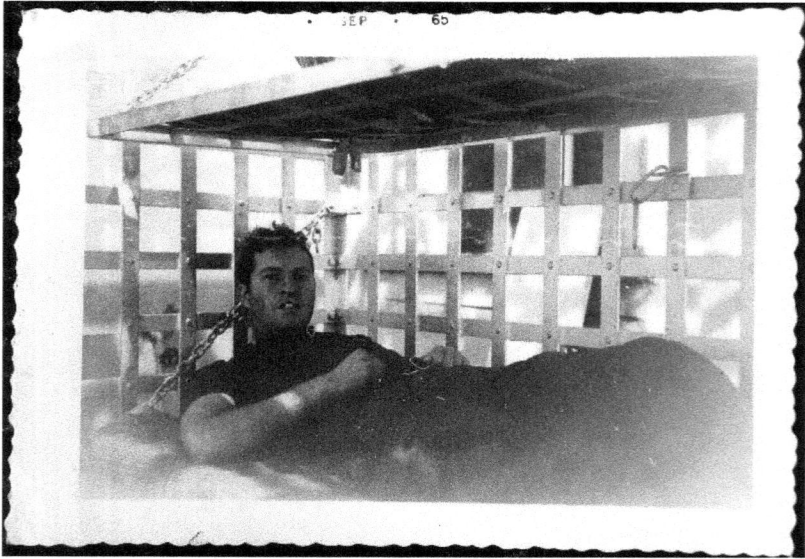

Bird City, Kansas
City Jail
(Free accommodations provided by the local Sheriff—"We'll just lock you up
for the night to keep you out of the rain.")

The Way Home

There is a point on all trips when the momentum turns from "onward" to "back". The definition of "back" is usually home.

Somewhere out on the high desert east of Reno, miles became more important than the stories they told, and recollections of thousands of miles are vague. I made other cross-country hitches over the next years and cetails of the return trips are intermingled. There were some fast cars, big trucks, and a night in the Bird City, Kansas, jail. I clearly recall my last ride on that 1964 trip. The guy picked me up somewhere in West Virginia and delivered me right to my parents' doorstep n Woodbridge, Virginia. It was a sunny Saturday afternoon in late June. My father was out back working in his garden. He grinned at me. I think my mother might have cried. I don't recall talking much about the trip to anybody. On some level I was aware that "back" and my folk's place were not the same thing with me anymore.

I noticed one commonality to all my solitary forays upon the nation's byways: All my journeys intersected with Carol. *Home* had become a person, not a place. I had been on a northwestern loop trip—it started when I dec ded Bismarck, North Dakota, seemed like a cool sounding place and just headed up that direction. Of course I stopped by St. Louis where Carol was staying at her mom's house preparing to begin a new job teaching in the nearby town of St. Charles. Just for the he:k of it, she convinced me to apply for admission to the University of Missouri at St. Louis. In some regards, I'm not the brightest fellow you've ever met, but even I was beginning to note the wonderful sense of inevitability to the course of my life and Carol's role in it. On the night before I left my parents' place for this road trip, my father, who I didn't even think noticed such things, asked me, "So, Robert, are you going out West to marry Carol?" I swear, it was like I was the last guy to figure it out.

Bismarck was just an overnight in a $2 hotel and then on up across Montana and Washington state. I had caught a couple of good rides with moving vans and had earned more money than I had spent. I must admit, the concept of perpetual motion had occurred to me. It was late August when I gave Carol a call from a phone booth in Vancouver. God the sound of her voice.

"And… by the way," she had told me, "you got accepted at the University."

A few days later, as I walked into St. Charles, Missouri, sometime after midnight, the local police picked me up, unburdened me of sharp objects and my belt, and locked me up in a cell in the basement of the courthouse. My previous incarceration had been in the Bird City Bird Cage in the back of the firehouse which had a decent bunk—and the next morning the police chief bought me breakfast. Much nicer, believe me. As I lay there in the St. Charles clink on a steel platform with a roll of toilet paper for a pillow, I thought maybe I had travelled enough for a while.

It was a fresh September morning—about seven a.m. I was standing on the front porch of Carol's little apartment wondering if I should wait a while before tapping when, suddenly, the door flew open. She nearly knocked me over rushing out with a big box of teacher stuff. She was all fresh and pretty in her schoolteacher dress—rushing out for the first day of what was to be an amazing forty-two-year career in education. I can imagine what a shock it was crashing into me out there on her porch. I was road-rugged, red-eyed weary, and smelling like a jailhouse but, even so, no kidding, she dropped her box, called out, "Robert!" and crushed me in her arms.

It seems you don't truly know where you are heading until you realize you have arrived.

The Nature of a Pure Gift

Carol made me promse not to pick up hitchhikers a few years back. It seemed hypocritical to me considering my history with the traveling thumb. But her argument was strong, "It's bad enough that you take off on cross-country drives, sleeping in the car and drinking in highway taverns. (This was a while back—when Budweiser was still a significant staple of my diet.) The least you can do to keep me from worrying myself to death is to not pick up strangers."

Well, she did have a good point there. The gift of her tolerance for the wanderlust inherent to the fellow she has spent most of her life with… and married, not once, but twice… is a marvel. She is a natural worrier and I am a natural wanderer—a strange melding of souls we are. With the advent of cell phones, well-lit interstate rest areas, and my State-of-Utah-issued, 37-state concealed weapon permit—I am able to keep in touch and honestly assure her of my relative safety upon the journeys I take.

I know among my roadside peers back on my early trips there surely was a share of rapists, serial killers, and rampant non-bathers (both we hitchers and they, the ride givers). But we didn't have methamphetamines, hedge-fund morality, or years of video-game violence roiling our psyches in 1964. Okay, I could live with an old hitchhiker's unpad debt to ramblers along the road. A degree of hypocrisy is pretty much a standard among the compromises requisite to becoming an adult. If calming a touch of her angst is achieved by denying the plea of an outstretched thumb, then so be it. Love makes pure self-absorption impossible. She loves me enough to embrace me at the door and wish me fine journeys and hardly weep at my departures—blessing me by decreasing the guilt as I heed the draw of distance. I love her enough to know I cannot travel without her blessing.

So, the other day, after sheepishly averting eyes and driving past a hitchhiker, I glanced in my rearview mirror to see this frantic young man shouting at me and flipping me off.

"One car too many…" I mused. "I know how you feel."

But then I thought about it and said aloud, "Actually, I don't know how you feel, you raging fool." (*Fool* as in, welcome to America, the well-armed land of road rage and hair-triggered reactions. I mean, I had nodded at the sons of bitches before they shot me in the sternum with a slingshot-launched marble back in Klamath Falls in 1964. What's this guy asking for out there flipping off a prospective, AK-47 madman?)

But it was true, and this is where a road tale becomes a philosophical tract. In some way, whether by outright choice or by the turns of fate, we are responsible for our own destinies. When the gazillionth driver cruised on past me on the side of the road out of that cold Oregon town, I still realized I was standing there as a result of my own wish. Well, yeah, I was a bit fatigued and in a less than cheery frame of mind and perhaps prone to an occasional mumble of disdain, but generally, I can honestly say I did not resent those who passed me by.

It was my decision to stand out in the elements and request the gift of free transportation. Each and every one of those drivers clear across the continent had the right to choose not to give me a ride. By accepting this state of no obligation, I never felt the urge to damn those who rejected me.

And when I think of it, such must be the nature of a true gift: a generous act bestowed without obligation.

Notes from an Old Man's Journey
East Central Missouri

Over fifty years ago, as a nineteen-year-old boy/man, I hitchhiked this stretch of U.S. Highway 50 across Missouri. Actually, I'm pretty close to the little town out where I ran into Marvin the Bugman. It's a ridge-riding, country-rolling road. In morning light, with autumn forest and the yet-green meadows and pumpkins for sale, I wondered about the fleeting turn of all these years and spoke out loud: I wonder. Have I lost my way?

Who could answer such a question? But introspection is seldom reasonable as it shakes doubt all down through the loosely-packed sediment of the strata of our times. God knows I have never quit the journey. I'm still out on this old road heading over the hills and piercing the mystery of the next curve for a glimpse of the unknown.

Part II

Some More Travel, People and Places: More Paths Taken

A Poem—Never Written

A poem—never written—
from a black-night train ride in Spain two years ago.

A slow train that swayed and clattered—
and I was alone in a crowd of sleep.
Outside in dotted, star-reflecting clusters
flashed in tree-broken glimpses, the
tiny lights that marked peoples' whole existences.

The Buddha and the Banjo-man
Taiwan / 1986

Most of the following Taiwan essays were included in my book, Adventure in the High Wind. *They seem right for this work. If you have read them before, no apologies. I've read them before and I still like them.*

Taiwan Sketches

In 1986, I traveled with a children's choir to Taiwan, Republic of China. My time-touched and sagely apathetic presence in the midst of such young, energetic, and talented people was the result of twenty-odd years of three-chord, "Cripple Creek," hillbilly banjo playing. I believe it was my fireworks accompaniment of "She'll Be Comin' Round the Mountain" performed with the choir at local concerts that cemented the relationship between this grizzled picker and the wholesome and harmonious chorale—and paid my ticket to twang internationally.

As my responsibility on this voyage was limited to showing up for performances and man-handling my banjo, my guitar, and sundry items of equipment associated with the amplification of my syncopated melodies, I enjoyed more freedom than the other adults in our entourage whose duties each included the twenty-four-hour supervision of two or three young people. In other words, while they were doing bed checks, I was doing night markets. It wasn't exactly fair, but then, to my knowledge, none of them could play the banjo either.

Following are written sketches taken from a green spiral notebook I carried on the trip, and recollections written since my return.

Taipei Morning

Six-thirty morning sunshine upon the ever-active streets. Wearing straw hats and big galoshes, the carwash ladies with buckets and hoses toil upon the Toyota fenders of taxicabs. The persistent, nasal buzz of motor scooters speaks through the alleyways and in droves at stoplights on the main boulevards. The rain last night was strong and the smell of sewage has diminished.

Children are coming out of apartment buildings and heading for school. First one little guy with his blue-shorts and white-shirt uniform steps into the alley and adjusts the weight of his backpack. He starts walking and others join him. At each intersection, as he waits for the crossing guards to blow their whistles and signal him to cross, more and more kids come: boys in their blue shorts, girls in blue skirts and white blouses. Everyone wears a backpack. Like the gathering of raindrops into streams, the flow of children increases at each intersection and moves on in a river of uniformed little students laughing and talking yet diligently progressing toward the wide gates of the school yard.

As I walk I, too, am swept along by the flood—carried by its current, only to beach myself as the river makes its final turn and disappears into the entryway of the four-story schoolhouse. There are teachers waiting and they smile at the children as they walk into the building.

At the gate a little girl with bright eyes and shining black hair climbs down from the back of her mother's bicycle and starts to run to join the others and disappear into the doorway. I take a picture. The mother doesn't approve and gives me a stern look. I apologize with my eyes, and she flashes a forgiving smile and rides back down the narrow street. There is the ringing of a bell. The street empties of child-sounds and movements, and returns to racing scooters, motorcycles, and horn-blowing taxicabs.

One morning I watched a man frying eggs on a gas grill mounted on a street cart. His business was located on a sidewalk where a small alley intersected with a wide and busy boulevard. I watched the artful movement of his spatula as he turned the eggs. There were people gathered about the cart patiently awaiting their breakfasts. His wife sold the eggs and pieces of bread while the man cracked more eggs and spread them upon the canvas of the black grill and, with grace and finesse, created a beautiful, yet never-finished painting.

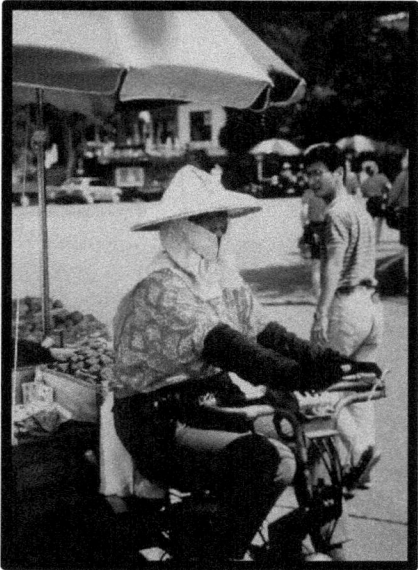

Travel Sketch: Taipei to Hualien City

This day there were holy moments along the train route down the east coast to Hualien. There were miles of shop-cluttered suburbs sprawling eastward along the rails out of Taipei. In all directions were concrete, cliff-dwelling apartment buildings where, upon balconies, imprisoned by trellises of metal, there were flowers growing and they were bright and beautiful and vividly alive. Beyond the city, in clearings cut from the dense, subtropical hillside vegetation, there were ornate and isolated shrines. In the eyes of laborers who toiled along the tracks with heavy burdens supported by bamboo shoulder poles, there were glimpses of the persistence of the human spirit. In town after town were stark, concrete-walled schoolyards filled with playing children. Beneath the bridges were women kneeling in shallow stream beds washing clothes. There was the great Pacific Sea and upon it were fishermen standing up in boats with skilled balance rowing through the roll of the near-shore surf.

Unfinished, Un-Mailed Letter

June 19, 1986
Hualien, Taiwan, ROC

Carol and Kristin,

There is no suitable place to begin any of this so I'll just tell what comes to mind. I'm having a few fine Taiwan Beers this afternoon, so bear with the condition of the mind from which these words are cast. A short time ago, while the troupe was resting up from a tour of a marble factory (needless to say, I passed on that one), I walked down to the harbor and, beyond the ships and the sea wall lay the Pacific Ocean. To the east! All my life this body of water has stretched ever westward, and now I have physically disproved the myth of its infinite reach. There is something disillusioning about this obvious discovery. It makes me wonder about the whole wide universe and its other shore.

Anyway, as I philosophically wandered this lovely sea town contemplating the clay feet of physical reality, dozens of people—two, three, even four at a time on single motor scooters—buzzed by me shouting with smiling faces, "Hello!" And I shouted back and I loved it. The Chinese people seem fascinated with me. Thus far on this trip I have yet to see a beard as big and fuzzy as mine on either Oriental or Occidental face. People stop me and ask to take pictures. I get to hang on to the prettiest girls while their boyfriends snap pictures of them with the fur-faced American. It's all very gracious and warm spirited. When they get their Fujicolor prints back, there will be the image of a genuine and heartfelt smile upon the face of the, hopefully, not too ugly American.

Most of the children with whom I have come in contact are shy and they giggle, covering their mouths with their hands. But they are not afraid, and we usually establish some gestured communication that neither they nor I fully understand, nor will ever forget.

There has been a major exception, though. Yesterday in Taipei, as the little ambassadors of song ingested course after

94

course of strange concoctions of il -defined flora and fauna back at the hotel dining room, I was blocks away, gleefully up to my eye sockets in a Big Mac. Just as I was finishing the last of my golden crisp French fries and considering another wonderful round of McDonald's grease and beef, a tiny little girl seated across from me caught sight of my wh skers. She immediately wrinkled up her cute little face, clamped shut her eyes, and, screeching like an exotic bird (or a male Chinese opera singer), buried her face in her mother's bosom—there to remain I assume, until long after I had made my hasty departure.

Today, as I walked back from the harbor and the ships and the great (though finite) ocean, among the rushing motor scooters and the pushcarts with fresh fruit and handmade jewelry, and beneath the green mountains that climb steeply to the west; I was feeling fantastic. I walked past an elementary school and a whole class of dinky little smiling kids wearing identical blue-and-white uniforms were pressed into an open doorway, and, in joyful discord, sang out a chorus of "hello's." I laughed and returned their greeting with a hearty "Hello!" and a wave and their arms were flying and they were laughing and even their teacher, in her spring-beige dress and her schoolgirl hair, smiled a pretty glance at me as she herded them back into the courtyard.

I'm going to walk up the street and buy a couple more beers. Perhaps I'll get back to this letter ater...

Snake Alley and the Red-Light Ladies

The prostitutes looked so young they could have been school girls.

Last night I walked down a red-light street and saw them there, dozens of them lined up in front of street-stall whorehouses. They wore fancy dresses like young girls used to wear to dances or to church on Easter Sunday. In white and lacy, long fancy dresses and with their gleaming black hair and red lipstick, they stood in regiment in the entryways along the dimly lit alley.

The red-light district is adjacent to the infamous and hideous street known as Snake Alley. There, shouting men, reminiscent of carnival barkers, amuse clusters of onlookers by first tantalizing and then cutting the heads off of live snakes and turtles and bleeding them to make blood potions to supposedly enhance the sexual potency of male customers. The bright red blood was lined up in shot glasses; cocktails were available for those who chose to dilute their poison.

It's all very convenient. A desperate man can down a shot of snake's blood to charge up his weakened libido; then just walk a short distance and hire a lady of the night to accommodate its discharge; and, finally, take a few more steps down another alley and visit a VD clinic to remedy the effects of its use. All of it is there in ghastly clarity, all of the rudiments of sex, devoid of humanity.

Earlier on the trip, while in Chiayi, we were accompanied by a group of students and their teachers from the Concordia School. The girls were all wearing pink blouses and gray jumpers. When they spoke their careful English to us, their eyes were bright with interest and they were so lovely in their modesty and in the spontaneity of their innocent faces. The teachers looked young as well, often only distinguishable from their students by the difference in their attire. When they spoke to me and we laughed together about small and polite matters, I perceived them in terms of a soft and sensuous grace, the pretty teacher-ladies of Chiayi.

And in that Taipei night scene, right down the block and off in a side alley from the sideshow decapitators of reptiles, could well have been sisters of the schoolgirls and teachers of Chiayi. They looked so young and, yet, so vacant—like mannequins dressed for a church party. Cruelly scrutinized by the hardened gaze of pimps and madams, they stood awaiting the whims of any passing creature. Their eyes were glazed and unseeing, deadened by drugs or fear or, perhaps, solely by the devastating effect of red-light shadows and the snake-blood taste upon the lips of drunken men.

Hung by string nooses and skinned while yet they quivered in the throes of death, were the victims of Snake Alley.

The Buddha-Man

The Buddha-Man sat cross-legged next to the curb of the filthy street. His shaved head was slightly bowed, his orange robe spread about him; he fervently mumbled a chant as his fingers ceaselessly worked their way through the infinite progression of the circular string of prayer beads he held in his hands. Passers-by dropped money into a bowl sitting on his lap, and each time he interrupted his words to give thanks with a nod. He never once looked up; his stoic countenance never varied.

I gave him money; he acknowledged my offering. I stood on the sidewalk behind him and listened to his mind.

While the intense confusion of the night market incessantly milled about us, we meditated. As the monk moved his beads and chanted the holy words of his ancient and life-disciplined technique, I breathed the measured air of my own meditation— inhaling slowly, deeply, exhaling through the extremities of my being through the soul-portals of my eyes, my mind.

I listened. I listened to the mind-spirit of the Buddha-Man.

I cannot write what I heard that Taipei-street-market night with its blowing horns and chattering merchants.

There are no words for such a silence.

... And

And there was Taroko Gorge with its narrow, one-lane road climbing up the chasm edge all the way to the clouds; and there were the throngs of people who crowded the stage in Koahsiung and again at Taipei, seeking autographs and expressing such appreciation with their smiles and their eyes; there was the heart-wide welcome of the County of Chiayi; and there was the giant Buddha near Tiachung, eighty feet high and black against the gray sky, where you can climb the spiral staircase innards, past the little incense shop and the religious displays, right up into the head and look out at the courtyard far below through the eight-inch-diameter nostrils of God.

And there was—in the movement, the smells, the sounds of the cities; the lushness and power of the mountains; the uniqueness of the cultures—a sense that the world is a vast and exotic place.

And, also, there was—in the laughter of the children, the friendliness of the people, and the view of daily life as a place of work and family and belief—a sense that this vast planet has elements which transcend diversity and connect us all as dwellers in a singular and spiritually unified human community.

Huayna Picchu, Sacred Mountain of the Incas
(from a Machu Picchu plaza)

No Words. Only Heart.

The Inca people of the Peruvian Andes did not worship sacred mountains as icons, representations of Deities. They worshiped Mountains, Sun and Moon, rushing Rivers, Condor, Puma, and Snake as Gods.

When I traveled to their cloud-city of Machu Picchu and climbed Huayna Picchu (why-nah-pee-chu), the great holy mountain that towers above, I trod upon the granite essence of Deity. I believe places of power exist independent of the frail contrivances of dogma we human superimpose upon them. The Mountain was neither Incan nor Christian. The Mountain was simply mighty.

Notebook Entries (2003):

(Agua Caliente, Peru/ Machu Picchu Bus / 6:00 a.m.)
Just a simple note: Today, as all days, I seek to clarify the blessings of the Gods.

But this day I will walk upon the sacred mountain of the Incas, Huayna Picchu.

Such a life I lead.

(Littleton, Colorado/ Einstein Bros. Bagels / 11:05 a.m.)

It has been a week now. Okay, I've flown the miles, I've slept away the weariness, I've rallied my immune system to confront mild intestinal havoc—when is my brain going to return from South America?

Perhaps, never.

Huayna Picchu is now a part of my soul.

The mystery of rising clouds and emerging mountains mightily breathes an enduring sense of tranquil power through my entire being. I am the Mountain. I am the Clouds. I am human spirit afoot upon the blessing of Earth. With subtle laughter, subtle tears... How I relish this day.

I'll tell what I can of my trek upon the sacred mountain.

103

* * * *

Somewhere in the vast body of my life's work, I wrote the following:

It takes exactly this long to get this far.

Forget accusations of procrastination, regrets over missed opportunities, the stress of goal-setting schedules. Each day is a precise intersection of what you are, what you know, and who you are—with the unique energies of this moment in the Universe. If you show up a day sooner for *now*, you won't know enough or *be* enough to handle the situation properly. Accept the internal pacing that drives your life and don't force it. When you can't find your car keys, you could be avoiding a wreck.

Path: A Sacred Journey

I guess luck is a major factor in the serendipity of certain of our encounters of *self* with opportunities for exceptional human, natural, or spiritual interaction. Luck, Divine intervention, karma—who can really say? I just know whatever we bring to each moment—our individual bundle of experience, knowledge, curse and blessing—takes all the hours of all the turning days of our existence to accumulate. And, on rare and amazing occasions, our mix of mind, flesh, and soul is ideally suited for wondrous encounter.

In Peru, I experienced one of the most significant intersections of my life's journey.

When I climbed the Incan sacred mountain, Huayna Picchu, decades of meditation, contemplation, study, chanting, listening, doubting, affirming, fearing the void while embracing the invisible— years of living the innocence and debauchery of the human path— all encountered a massive stone spire of cloud and might and mystery.

While the other dozen trekkers who clung to the slanted rock of the peak wrapped themselves in ponchos—a German fellow popped open an umbrella (I mean, right on the forehead of God the guy was hovering under a powder blue parasol).

I sat apart from the diverse scatter of strangers and let the precious touch of rain soak me. The men and women, young folks, mostly in their 20's I'd guess, had gathered there from about the globe to check out the view of Machu Picchu somewhere far beneath, lost in morning clouds. With the exception of a couple of more contemplative sorts, they were a giddy bunch—prone to chatter and riffs of laughter. Thankfully, they were also periodically awed by vistas of vast mountains and enwrapping clouds and expressed pauses of rich silence.

I don't criticize these hardy folks. It's not an easy climb and each of us has our own purpose in a day's journey.

Sometimes we are *tourists*—out for the view, for the entertainment of nature and culture—*vacationers*. At other times we are *travelers*, out to absorb, to seek, beyond the next turn and over the next rise, another mile's glimpse of an infinite road. For the most part, my companions up there were on a hike; I was on a holy pilgrimage. I had made the hour's ascent in profound isolation and, other than a laughing acknowledgment of the applause I received upon crawling to the summit (I guess they had never expected anyone as ancient as myself, ruddy-faced and hoary-bearded to join their youthful ranks), I kept a polite distance from the others. When with companions we tend to engage in witty banter and futile attempts at verbalizing unspeakable awe. Though we may walk upon the essence of a God, we giggle about the rain.

A sacred journey, regardless of the crowds about us, must be a solitary trek.

It's all about timing. Some people may come to such a magical encounter too soon in their journey. They may fail to realize that what is sacred about an Incan God-of-a-Mountain is as simple as the dazzling sense of fear and beauty resplendent in its aura. Some arrive too late, too entrenched in certainty of dogma or concrete reality to give primordial Deity access to their beings.

Gripping the slick wet stone, I physically resisted gravity's fatal will while, spiritually, with uninhibited, blissful willingness, I released my soul to the exhilarating, transcendent beauty of the moment. I soared free and knew the enlightenment of fifty-nine years of breath and bruise and song and bliss and step and stumble's intersection with the immortal energies of a sacred mountain.

Resting in the clouds.

The ancient trail up Huayna Picchu.

Smiling farewell to the others who chose to await clearing clouds and better photos, I began carefully making my way down the hundreds of ancient and often treacherous steps. I was alone, dripping wet, engulfed in a bone-deep weariness of both flesh and heart, and, yes, I was genuinely giddy. Feeling an uncanny sense of excitement in my entire being that time and miles have not begun to erase—a joy that resonates as a verging of laughter, a brink of sweet sadness—I was prone to spontaneous outbursts of shouts and chuckles while grasping the cable and rope safety lines that kept me from flying right off the side of the mountain and on down through the mist. It was with such exuberance as I negotiated a switchback that I encountered two people coming up the mountain. Believe me, they looked a bit startled at the sight of a 200-pound geezer veritably clicking heels as he swept down the path toward them.

I came to a graceless halt just short of crashing right into the hapless hikers. I grinned; they gaped. Then, I broke the stalemate of my wild eyes and their wide eyes with a near-bellowed greeting in my finest English, "Hello!"

In their polite Spanish, the young couple replied, "Hola."

With gestures and traces of common language, they conveyed the question, "What is it like up there?"

I hesitated, seeking an appropriate response. Then I realized there was no language barrier frustrating my reply. There clearly was no language to speak. I smiled broadly and shrugged my shoulders. In crude Spanish I said, "… no palabras… solamente… corazón."

The man smiled at his companion and said, "No words. Only heart."

View from the Head of a God

RN
2/2012

Dancing with the Gods

Spirit Mountain.

A holy place, distinct among the stark rock peaks rising in a great ridge above the Colorado River in Southern Nevada. It is a white promontory, the mountains that shoulder it north and south are dark. Native peoples throughout the region have worshiped spirits that dwell there for untold ages, since long before the European invasion. It was known by peoples as far away as the Mississippi River cultures hundreds of miles east. I know nothing of the Gods to whom they direct their prayers and rituals. The place is sacred; the myths, hallowed though they may be, were not the object of my journey.

I didn't go to the mountain to encounter ancient Indian Gods. I went there because the place is sacred. I went there to encounter my own Gods.

I'll try to explain, to you and to myself, what goes on when this pilgrim dismisses a serious agnostic streak and opens mind and heart to a marvelously irrational spiritual reality.

My old college bud, A.D. Hopkins, told me about the holy place down toward Laughlin during a visit to Las Vegas in May of 2012. I wrote him the following after spending an amazing night at the foot of the mountain.

A.D., after over 40 years of big-time newspaper reporting, is a major stickler for detail. He responded with a bit of a correction of my use of the term "Gods". He wrote:

Glad you had a good time down there with the gods, or God. I think only the creator is supposed to live there, even if they recognize other gods. Pretty sure they believe in other spirits, but don't know if spirits are considered gods— in my own religion now that I mention it, let alone, Colorado River Tribes.

I'm sure he's right. He usually is.

But, he's dead wrong in taking the capital letter 'G' away from my Gods. As I stood beneath the celestial-sized dome of St. Peter's in Rome, the chant mumble of Holy Rites vibrated from ornate alcoves bestowing blessings upon ardent believers. I am not Christian, much less am I a Catholic. What I encountered in that massive basilica was not the God of Abraham nor was it the Christ of Peter. Nor was it the dogma of Paul or the 'infallible' dominion of the Pope.

Suspended in the vastness of Michelangelo's marvel of stone architecture, I felt a significant presence of focused spirit that resonated within me.

As I stood before a display case at a museum of antiquities in Taipai, Taiwan, and beheld a tiny glass bead purported to contain a fleck of ash from the cremated body of The Buddha, I didn't become a Buddhist. But what I felt was a twenty-five-hundred year sweep of compassion as real as the embrace of a loved one.

As I climbed the Incan scared mountain, Huayna Picchu, I did not do so as a potential convert to myths of the Andes. I sought, in this exotic and revered site, open access to the awesome *Wonders* that impact each day I live.

I embraced the sacred bond existent between an ancient culture and a holy mountain, and returned to a Twenty-First Century reality forever changed by the experience.

Bless the peoples of Andean Peru, I honor their beliefs, just as I do so the ways of the St. Peter's Catholics. My personal experience has led me to believe that ritual and dogma are temporal and human incidentals to phenomena that are truly sacred. With open heart and unflinching acceptance of the poetic, the metaphoric validity of diverse human endeavors to explain the explicable, whether holy icon or spiritual mountain or epiphany of sunset out on the end of Santa Monica Pier, there is Universal Truth to be garnered from matters and places sacred.

With mantra-rhythmic, five-stringed banjo prayers plunked and shouted from the desert floor to the Cosmic arching sky, the capital 'G' Gods that swirled the dust with me, and sang indescribable harmonies to the solitary sanctity of my night at the base of Spirit Mountain were as real as any known to the history or moment of my species.

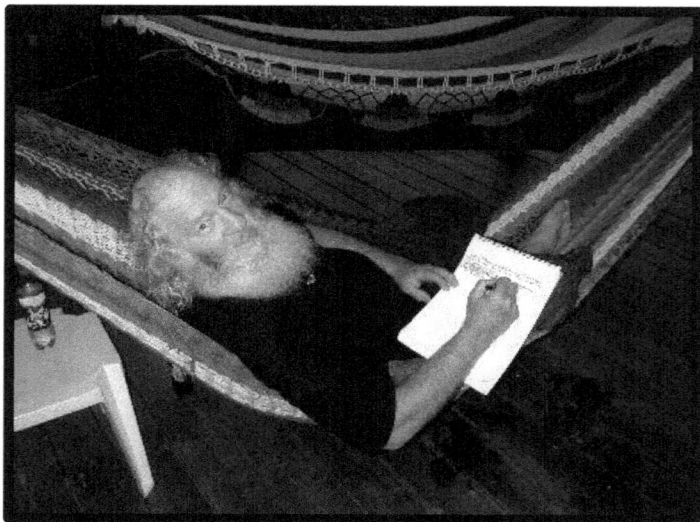

Poet in a Hammock—a good match,
Anthony's Key
Roatán, Honduras / 2005

Roatán / December, 2005

I should preface this tale of a magical island and the blue-green waters that surround it by telling you that I float like a brick. Sure, I can swim, but it's not pretty. Fully outfitted with scuba gear, I once took a complementary lap in a dive shop swimming pool. I bubbled along near the bottom for some time. It wasn't particularly scenic but I did enjoy the unique experience of breathing underwater. When I emerged at the far end of the pool, the instructor who had accompanied me on my fifty-foot foray into the subaquatic depths smiled broadly and said to the others in the class, "My, Mr. Nichols is relaxed. He really took his time didn't he?"

I just grinned and said, "Honest. That was as fast as I go."

I love water, but am pretty much of a land animal. I've come to accept this fact. While in water-treading situations where others calmly chat and enjoy the freedom of natural buoyancy, just occasionally giving a little kick to maintain their status as air breathers bobbing upon the surface, I tend to require a great deal of thrashing about just to avoid sinking.

This limitation just adds to the intensity of the experiences I'm about to share with you.

Consider a simple idea. One that justifies investment of time and resource in the seeming impracticality of natural and aesthetic experience:

We do not create beauty;
beauty creates us.

Open and perceptive (artful, if you will) interaction with nature is the most primal and essential source of our humanity. Deny significant exposure to sunsets, forests and peaks, puppies, raging oceans, unsullied breezes, free-flowing laughter (yes, puppies and laughter are as much a part of nature as Arizona canyons and Yellowstone geysers) and you may well wither into bitter cynicism or, at a minimum, end up working, sleeping, watching a lot of bad television and trying to call it a life. Encounters with natural wonder are not optional frills. They are crucial wellsprings of spiritual and physical nourishment. It is possible to be *saved* by a beautiful backyard garden or intimate harkening to neighborhood birdsongs, but a blockbuster dose of pink dolphins a-play in the mirror-smooth waters of an Amazonian sunrise or the rumble-sighing rhythms of surf-song explosion upon a sea cliff can be what it takes to blast the apathy right out of you and replenish your sulking soul.

Kind of makes you want to peel out the plastic and head on down to your travel agent, doesn't it?

I'll give you a hint of what a week in Roatán did for my humanity.

The Sea

I'll tell you of the fish of this warm clear sea. As one who delights in the colors and textures, the interactive biological wonder, the eco-marvel of the surface of this planet, my visit to a natural coral garden was life expanding.

As part of our snorkel vacation package at Anthony's Key Resort, my wife Carol, adult daughter Kristin, and I began our encounter with the sea off a large boat out by the reef that surrounds Roatán. The two of them did fine, but my experience, due to the choppy waters, my hairy face and leaky mask, and general aquatic ineptitude proved to be more a time of struggle than liberation. We all wore lightweight flotation vests, but, as my ladies took to the sea like a pair of ambling dolphins, I kept flopping over, belly up like a dead fish, eyes cast despairingly to the blazing blue sky, uttering vile epithets and hooting such phrases as, "Next year we'll go to Siberia."

The following day I was perfectly willing to rename our "snorkeling vacation" a "sea kayak vacation," or, even better, a "hammock vacation." But Carol wouldn't hear of it. Years earlier, she had scuba-dived in nearby waters and was determined that I not miss out on the wonders she knew were awaiting me if only I would master some basic techniques of snorkeling. After a session of mutter and self-pity, I agreed to try again. "Maybe this time, rather than looking up to see your reedy little air tube steadily gliding toward the briny horizon, I might have the pleasure of your company in this ordeal."

I was a little testy about the subject, but garnered not an iota of sympathy from my companions. A round of "toughen up" in two-part harmony finished off the last of my moping. I did manage to get Carol to agree to stay by my leaden side and the three us gathered gear and headed for the water-taxi dock.

Bailey's Key is a thin thicket of vegetation, harsh rock and, thankfully, sand that juts out toward the Caribbean, forming part of the enclosure in which semi-independent dolphins dwell. It is the site where we humans are provided a fantastic opportunity to interact with our aquatic counterparts. Standing the shallow waters, gently hugging a 250-pound mammalian torpedo and realizing the intelligence and docile marvel of these animals can be a joyous experience for any who are willing to forgo our *Homo sapians* egos and realize we're all just a bunch of cousins here on Planet Earth. And, hey, these dolphins are actually kissin' cousins, at that.

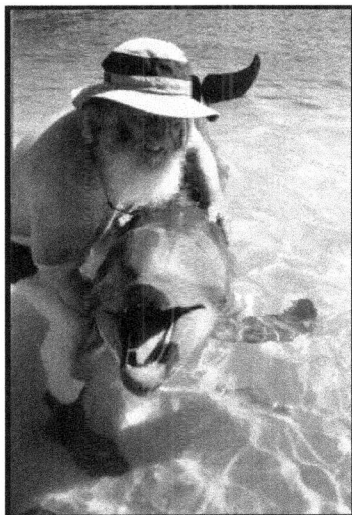

We waved at the flippered friends we had met the previous day during the "Dolphin Encounter" included in our deal, and headed along a short sandy path to the west side of Bailey's Key where the coral grows in shallow waters alee of the northeast storms.

It was beautiful there with the sand and the water and the lush green land of tropical highlands to the south and the arcing reach of the ocean spread forever to the north. A near-perfect place to make transition from land to sea. *Near* perfect, I say, not perfect.

The current, the big clumsy flippers we wore, the abrasive deceit of coral clumps upon the rock-strewn bottom: so fragile, delicate, and painfully harsh—it wasn't easy to get into the swirl of the shallows and cast off for the depths.

I helped Carol and Kristin clear the shore and float out to the deep clear water. I watched as my dear people, with faces down and yellow snorkels up, gently stirred the waters and drifted away.

Okay, I thought, here we go again—another round of splash, choke, gasp and then back to the shin-banging torment of the shore. Just like usual.

I'm such a good sport. I stumbled in, expecting the worst.

But, wonder of days, this was not to be. Somehow, once afloat beyond the shallows, my mask fit snugly over the mess of my moustache, my breathing tube abounded with gurgle-free air, and, suddenly, the angst of the struggle forgotten, I honestly felt as if I were flying. Beneath me, the coral forest grew in intricate complexities of chamber and chasm, fan and stem. And, donned in display of brilliant color beyond all extremes of terrestrial spectra, fish in gentle patterns went about their fish business oblivious to either me or to the marvel of their own magnificence. Like an eagle buoyed by currents of rising air, I floated upon the sky-water blessing as below me unique dimensions of remarkable hue and motion and grace revealed to me the humbling wonder of worlds beyond my experience.

Carol, from somewhere out toward the aforementioned arcing horizon (so much for her assurances of staying by her man), shrieked and shouted with joy, the delight of her nose-to-nose near collision with passing wild dolphin. Eureka!

Kristin spotted a barracuda.

And, from darkened depth of a felt-pure void, there rose beneath me a flight, a school of exquisitely blue and surreally sedate fish in random array giving visual caress to my awe, turning as one into the sun-glow revelation of their vivid translucence, and, then, disappearing forever into mystery.

And, thus was the sea.

Captain Emerald's Craft

Victor loves his home. His island.

Carol had discovered him on the web while searching for Cactus Juice in preparation for the trip. Most of the comments she read from people who had traveled in Roatán were something like, "... closest thing to paradise on earth except for the miserable bugs." It's the tropics, you know. Any place on the planet I've visited that is lush and warm and fertile is also rainy and humid and infested. It's nature's way. It could be worse. I've been to places that are stark and scorched and just as infested. Bugs are almost everywhere as are the salves and sprays and smoky little burners intent upon rebuffing the inevitable assaults of scurrying, buzzing, slithering insects. The ideal insect repellant would be non-carcinogenic, organic, pleasantly scented, quickly absorbed and, oh yeah, EFFECTIVE!

(Does anyone really know what DEET is? Spooky, I'd say.)

The closest modern-day ooze to the bug-balm Adam rubbed on Sweet Eve's back in Eden may well be a product called Cactus Juice. It contains no mysterious toxins or chemical progeny of Agent Orange, has a nice citrus smell, doesn't leave a creepy crust on your skin and, might even dissuade a few of the hordes of ravenous critters with whom we share the ecosystem of Paradise.

While Carol browsed anecdotal recommendations for surviving the Roatán experience with bliss intact, she found glowing reports of both Cactus Juice and of a local fellow who gives wonderful tours. She tracked down a Denver dive shop as a distributor of Cactus Juice, and after a few friendly exchanges of e-mail, booked the services of Victor Bodden who agreed to meet us at Anthony's Key Resort for a day's cab trek of his island.

We connected on one of the delightfully rainy days of our week and off we went. Victor was great, a calm and articulate man who sincerely enjoys showing people around his homeland.

The whole tour was fantastic, but the best of it was our experience with Captain Emerald and the mangrove tunnels.

We had driven slowly through Punta Gorda, the ancient slave village where descendants of the Garifuna people have dwelled for centuries since abandonment by their British slave masters back in 1792. Carol wanted to see about local crafts and, also, after checking with Victor to assure she wouldn't insult anyone, she wanted to give the children there some small toys and candy canes she had hauled from home. Victor stopped in the dirt street in front of shoreline cottages and tapped his horn. A lank and serious looking man appeared in a window and then came out with a nice collection of necklaces and pendants he had made from wood and bone and bead. Deals were made through the car window, money exchanged for art, and then Carol motioned to the man's small sons who had been watching from the yard. She gave them wonderful little toy metal cars and treats, and for the little girl who had come from next door she had candy and a doll. The children were truly pleased and all grinned and said, "Thank you." We continued on along the sand-dirt street and children appeared magically from the rain and rubble and lit our day with such marvelous smiles as Carol shared her simple gifts.

Our destination on the south shore of the island was the town of Oak Ridge. As we slowly dropped from hilltop down into the harbor, a group of men sprang from a shelter where they had been waiting out the rain and mobbed our cab. Victor rolled down the window and in rapid Creole English negotiated for a water taxi to take us through the mangrove tunnels up the coast west of the town. The rains had been coming in waves all day, some of them quite heavy and he insisted that the motor canoe have some form of tarp. A man assured Victor he could accommodate us for $25 and an agreement was made.

We parked in a lot adjacent to the water and followed a tall lean black fellow with a woven green cap through a narrow alley and out to the wharf where his small craft was moored. "Wait, wait," he said. "I will dry off the seats." We stood in awe, assessing the vessel hired to transport us across the storm-gray waters and through a maze of tangled roots and hidden channels. It was a narrow and long canoe of indeterminate vintage—not so much ageless as aged. The promised canopy was four bamboo sticks supporting what looked to be a tablecloth from an Italian restaurant. Plastered about the inside were dozens of little signs giving information about the island, naming landmarks, making claims like "Very Romantic." Quaint decor, perhaps; or possibly to conceal sealed leaks and seam cracks. The sign closest to the pilot read "God is my guard."

I'd say.

The entire boat had the appearance of tenuous fragility sustained by ingenuity and faith.

We loved it.

As we waited, I thought back to another visit to this island, and, especially of a different sort of boat.

The first time the three of us were on Roatán was a couple of years earlier as a four-hour stopover on a Caribbean cruise. Carol and Kristin had gone off for a dolphin encounter at Anthony's Key while I opted to just wander around the harbor town of Coxen Hole. I recall the Honduran cop at the border gate didn't even have a holster for his gun. He just had a .38 revolver stuck in his belt. I guessed their homeland security budget wasn't as plentiful as ours up in the U.S. I walked the pier to the shore and then followed the gentle curve of the beach road for a ways. There were houses, some would call them shacks, all up along the hillside and small shops and beautiful little kids walking home from school. I stopped and looked back across the sand beach and the smooth waters to where our ship, the *Norwegian Sun*, gleamed—an eleven-story palace, massive and luxuriant. There were hints of music and child-play laughter and scents of spicy foods. I heard mothers calling their children, and before us all there was the immortal beauty of the sea. And then... there was the great gaudy ship and its invading mob of thousands of tourists, yours truly included. Juxtaposed there with plywood hovels and lean-to poverty, the ship looked bigger than the whole town. I gave all the pocket change I had to the kids who traipsed along with me as I headed back to my floating First-World barge. Something about the scene made me angry, though I didn't really want to know why. The word "ostentatious" kept burping up into my throat like a bad cucumber. I waved goodbye to the kids... well, actually, once I ran out of money, for fear that they might devour me, I had started jogging briskly away— my farewell was on the fly. The scrawny little cop at the pier stopped me and, with a hand on the grip of the pistol carelessly suspended by his belt, demanded I give him a dollar to let me pass. I told him to get the hell out of my way, which he did.

And then, two years later, in the warm drizzle as we three awaited permission to board our craft, I reached out and shook the hand of our boatman and asked his name.

He smiled and said, "Emerald. Captain Emerald."

Captain Emerald and Kristin

126

I thought of the *Norwegian Sun* and laughed joyfully as we gingerly stepped down into the boat.

The less adventuresome would have politely declined the opportunity and retreated to the safety of the cab. But we trusted Victor. He obviously loved his life and his family and he wasn't likely to endanger his own self any more than ourselves by getting us lost or sunk in the water jungle, would he?

Hey, why travel the world if you're afraid to take a bit of a risk?

Carefully balancing his human cargo with Carol and Kristin side-by-side in the middle, Victor up front and me in front of him, Captain Emerald pulled the rope and the old engine began to *puck-a-ta*. We untied the lines from the wharf cleats and with rev of rhythmic chatter and wheeze, began our voyage.

What fun.

"I really like your boat," I said as we cleared the landing and headed out across the harbor with its fishing boats and canneries and brightly colored shore shacks and stark churches and part-time palaces of the rich.

We stopped at a wharf-side gas station for a gallon or two and then steadily progressed across the inlet on through the narrow gap and out to the calm sea waters protected by the reef. My lovely ladies grinned back at me and Victor nodded from the front. The captain pointed out the sights and answered my questions in Caribbean English, clear and almost musical.

We turned inland up a channel and immediately understood what a mangrove tunnel was. The mangrove trees grew in dense groves in shallow tidal waters with most of their twisted labyrinth of roots exposed. The trees were thick and, arching above the water course, they entangled leaf and snaky vine forming a dark and dank tunnel of vegetation through which we, *puck-a-ta—puck-a-ta*, glided by will of craft, skill of Captain Emerald and, of course, *Guard of God*.

Out of darkness and into the cloud-bright light we emerged into a small bay where, we were told, boats were brought to wait out hurricanes. Then, breaching the facade of greenery, we plunged back into the tunnels.

In the convoluted crotches of the tangled roots there dwelled, brilliant and jewel-like, red crabs. And all up and down the black bark there were strange insects—triangular and elongated and oozy and crisp, armor plated and pincher ready, slug-gooey, leggy and winged, grotesque and beautiful, most of which seemed to scurry toward, not away from us.

"Look," called Victor from the bow. "Someone killed a snake!"

And there, bloated and fatally coiled, floated the corpse of a thick serpent, pale white in the sheen of the river ripples.

Captain Emerald said, "But, don't worry. There are no poisonous snakes on our island."

"Well, that's a relief."

And Victor concurred. "Not a single poisonous snake."

Carol and Kristin, who are both dreadfully afraid of all legless, tongue-flicking reptiles, seemed somewhat relieved as well.

I said, "So, what kind of snake is that dead one over there?"

"That one's a boa," said the captain.

"Oh."

Puck-a-ta-puck-a-ta the old motor sounded through the black flood of shadows. And then, *puck-a-ta—puck…* whoosh, pop… and nothing. In silence we drifted. I could hear the sound of Carol's eyelids stretching open.

Captain Emerald laughed and said, "No worry. I shut it off myself. I want to show you something." The boat stopped and, grabbing the moist roots, we pulled it back a few yards and he pointed out a large crab of such a deep and glowing red that it veritably glowed from its nest in the ebony tangle.

Then, after maybe six or eight or a dozen or so pulls on the rope, the old engine shuddered to life and on we went.

When we bade our able captain goodbye later that afternoon, I felt as if we had bonded. At least I didn't embarrass myself, my family, or my homeland by hugging him.

128

Rain, Cheese Quesadillas and
Passive Bliss

It was the third day of our tropical adventure when the great rains came. Rains like I have seldom known. Wonderful, warm and drenching downpours. Cloud banks and seascape were furiously black and, in powerful contrast, the raging white surf curled wildly over the reef creating the surreal illusion of a monochrome world. I thought of the iridescent creatures harbored in the coral depths.

Of course, along the wharf or waiting at the taxi boat slip, most of what we heard from our fellow vacationers were complaints about the weather. Foisted upon shallow minds by a conspiracy of weather persons and desert land-deal shysters is the erroneous myth that sunshine is requisite for good times. Give me all the seasons, all the shades and textures of time and tempest, all the threat and bounty, ravage and blessing of Earth's dangerous and beneficent bag of tricks. It was the tropics in December—what the locals quaintly refer to as "rainy season." If you don't like rain, then, I say, vacation with the lizards of Death Valley. We loved the squalls and the winds howling through the louvers of our cabana. Who could gripe, it blew the lousy mosquitoes away.

The roiling sea stirred up the bottom and made sand soup of the shallow waters off the key and nixed notions of snorkeling, so Carol and I took a cab into the nearby settlement of West End. There, we discovered the quintessential, sleepy little Caribbean fishing village / tourist enclave with streets of sand, shops and restaurants, canopy-covered cantinas and a casual parade of barefoot locals and bargain-hunting Americans and Europeans on holiday. Boat docks and dive shops lined the beach.

After an hour, laden with a cache of small carvings and dangles of jewelry, Carol was satisfied she had sufficiently enriched the economy of Honduras and we sat on the porch of a bar nibbling the best cheese quesadilla I had ever eaten. Sheets of rain pummeled the tin roof and puddled the potholed street before us. The grumbling masses were muted, trapped in pockets of shelter up and down the road; the waitress was friendly and laughed at my jokes;

and beside me at the table, with hair all soaked and dangling and clothes soggy and drooping, was my wife and favorite person in the world. We hardly spoke. We just sat there slowly eating the rain-sprayed tortillas, sipping our cokes, and grinning in utter and blissful amazement at where we were.

End

The rains had passed. The sky and sea were clear and calm. My other favorite person in the world, my daughter Kristin, was out on the deck a-sway in the meditation of gentle breeze and a good hammock. To the west, the sun set in glorious glow. It was the last light of the last day of our week in Roatán. Carol and I were laughing about nothing and stuffing wet stuff into plastic bags and cramming them into suitcases.

When the time is up on a good trip, I am always ready to go home. Travel is not for escape; it is for nourishment.

PART III

Darkness Along the Path: The Persistence of Prejudice

1961
1962
1963
1965
1968
1999

January 20, 2017

One can hardly write about racism in in this country without mention of the "N" word.

I know the importance of political correctness when it establishes social norms of sensitivity and compassion. I have threatened life and limb of fools who have cast about the ugly word "retard" in proximity to my daughter. If we are made more aware of the harsh repercussions of our unthinking utterances and actions: *good*. Such heightened sensitivity can create a safer world for us all.

But, believe me, being disingenuously careful about political correction fools no one. The dark truths that lie in our hearts trump attempts at semantic camouflage.

In the context of the following events, the word is *Nigger*.

The Color of Reality

It wasn't until I started gathering material for this book that I realized the recurring theme of racism in the stories of my life.

I'm about as mainstream Caucasian/American male as blood and circumstance could concoct. English-Celtic dad, European Celtic mom; suburb reared, Protestant baptized, educated in segregated elementary and junior high schools. You'd think I would be thrilled by the radical conservative turn in American politics. I exactly fit the profile of the ideal citizen these neo-Nazis and White supremacists cater to. Heil.

Man, is this all wrong.

But, I'd better face the truth of the times in which I have lived— the truth of the society of the fifties in which my basic assumptions were established. You see, in those years, almost all of us White people were racists, sexists, and self-righteous xenophobes. We didn't use the "N" word n our household. We were taught the manners of *ladies first*, we were gradually despising the Germans less (it took a little longer with the Japanese—they're not White). We acted nice, but the truth was we did not consider Blacks to be equal in ability or potential to Whites—still only about 3/5 of a human-being as counted by the original U.S. Constitution, I suppose. We didn't believe women to be equal to men in intelligence, strength, or judgement. And (God bless White America) we were obviously morally and militarily superior among all the nations of the world.

I'm not talking about Deep South, whip-and-lynch oppression. This was middle class, suburban America. (I was convocated into the Webster Groves Presbyterian Church in 1960. Other than Mr. Wilkerson, the janitor, I don't recall a person of color in the entire congregation.) We didn't hate or fear Blacks, we just never thought of honestly respecting them as equals.

Think about it. If you are over sixty, you probably can recall the shock of seeing Black people in TV commercials for the first time in the late 60s.

In 1954 the Supreme Court ruled public school segregation to be unconstitutional.

In 1959 when I started high school I entered the first integrated classroom in my educational career.

In 1960 my family moved to the Northern Virginia suburb of Woodbridge and it was segregation all over again. And, I'll admit, it was somewhat of a relief for me. Less stress—many of the Blacks in my old high school were a confrontational bunch and prone to violence, though, not without some cause.

I remember a day in the locker room after gym class. Without even thinking about it, natural segregation had occurred when we chose our lockers and all the Whites were on one side and the Blacks on the other. There was this obnoxious White kid, I'll call him Terry. I never did like him. He was alone in a corner of the room when three of the Black guys walked over from their enclave and shoved him against the metal lockers with a crash.

I watched.

They slapped him around some and he started begging and apologizing. It seems, just joking you know, he had called one of the brothers Aunt Jemima.

I just stood there watching.

The Blacks left. Terry wasn't hurt, just shaken up. To this day I have conflicting feelings about the incident. Terry had it coming, but I did nothing to even the odds against him. Coward? I don't know.

Anyway, at my new school such moral dilemmas were less likely to challenge my good opinion of myself.

Times were really starting to stir in the South. At the end of my junior year, June 1961, the principal gathered the whole student body for a mass announcement out in front of the school. Standing on the tailgate of a pickup truck (no kidding, a pickup truck) he told us:

"We don't want this, but it isn't up to us anymore. They're making us do this. Starting next school year, we're being forced to begin integrating our school district. The Federal Government is requiring this and we can't do anything to stop it. This is the way it is, and in September I want you to know there could be some protest, some catcallers and the like. We need to ignore it and go about our business."

136

Of course, I knew this was ridiculous. "Forced" to treat people decently. What a crock. They called it "State's Rights." Nonsense, it was White supremacy.

And, by the way, the dreaded integration of our precious fortress of Caucasian purity took place without a single "catcall." But then, why wouldn't it? There were over 800 students at the high school and the gradual process of diverse inclusion began that fall with the enrollment of one little eighth-grade girl. That's right. One brave Black child—my God how scared she must have been—in all the halls of that bastion of rednecks. I rarely saw her—and when I did she was always plowing through the shuffling hordes alone. I hated it. I knew it was wrong. I did nothing to befriend her.

In August of 1963 I heard of a march. It was the summer between my freshman and sophomore years at the 100% segregated University of Richmond. (I knew that was wrong too—but it was the South where most institutions of *higher* learning were still segregated.) Martin Luther King was coming to Washington to protest the status quo of hatred and discrimination that was the United States of America. It was to be a mass gathering of tens of thousands of protesters marching for "Jobs and Freedom."

And, finally, I did something. I hitchhiked the twenty miles into the city and joined in on the most amazing spectacle I had ever seen. Over 200,000 of us walked from the Washington Monument to the Lincoln Memorial that day. We sang, we joined arms—I didn't know there were that many Black people in the world and there I was, Bob-the-White-Guy giddy among the righteous throng. I had been apprehensive the night before. Mainstream media had warned that such a huge assemblage of protesters (*i.e.* Negros) would surely result in mayhem and destruction. As soon as I got there and sensed the mood of the day I never felt the least threatened. Martin Luther King's credo of non-violence was vibrant that day. (I believe the only arrest made was of an American Nazi Party zealot who got frustrated and pissed from his soapbox.)

I was there for the speeches from the steps of the Lincoln Memorial. (Actually, for a while, up in a tree along the Reflecting Pool until a cop made me get down.) It was wonderful, and though I couldn't understand a word of Martin Luther King's dream—it was all echo and cheer—I was there and it was a significant moment in the history of the world. I could feel it.

137

A Man Died That Night: Ole Miss Riots
(Oxford, Mississippi, 1962)

A man died that shameful night.
In the souls of thousands
there should be pain.

He wore a heavy moustache—
a rounded goatee,
his eyes projected concern
(behind dark-rimmed glasses).
His name was Paul.
He was a newspaper reporter
covering the outrageous notion
that James Meredith, a Black man,
might study
among the Mississippi Whites
at Ole Miss.

They say it was righteousness
for which they fought that night—
killed that night.
Yes, the right of a state
to discriminate against
its slaves—
or rather, emancipated slaves
(still enslaved by bigotry and
curse of statute and ethos).

I read about it in the paper.
There were reports on television.
Films of the riot
showing thousands—
a great mob swarming

wildly through the tear-gas clouds.

How the fiends gasped,
screaming their wrath
and blindly hurling their hatred
into the night.

And from my perspective,
so far away
(in a dormitory room at Richmond)
I read *The Newsleader*
and *Times Dispatch*.
They listed a name (with a small picture).
They say he was thirty.
They spoke of a two-sided question,
as if the voice
of a murderous mob of racists
bore credence
in some ongoing intellectual
discussion.

James Meredith, he went on
to become a lawyer.

And Paul,
Paul Guihard,
a French journalist covering
the American Civil Rights conflict,
was murdered by the righteous throng.
(Shot in the back, actually.)

And so it was that ugly night
of October 1, 1962
when tear gas
and Federal troops
accomplished
what reason

and compassion
and true democracy could not.

James Meredith entered graduate school.
Paul Guihard went home in a coffin.

Summer, 1963

Sweet grapes, river wound
through green summer mountains,
surf-moon—pounding, curling pools
of yellow night,
white-pure hearts splashing red
on curly black Sunday-school hair.

From *The Messenger*, Fall *1963* / University of Richmond

The Hole Truth
(1965)

I'm not proud of this.

It doesn't trouble me like the acts of cowardice, ill-spoken words, and thoughtless deeds I have committed over the years. It doesn't make me crawl inside or cringingly turn from myself. But it was terrible and, though it happened back when I was a twenty-year-old kid, I have never found the means to resolve its implications. You see, what happened was wrong, terribly wrong, but I can't say that, given the identical circumstances, I wouldn't respond today exactly as I did back then. I think, somehow, the incident with which I was so directly involved did more to define the world than it did to define me.

It was the summer of 1965, the summer that divided my motorcycle spring from my matrimonial autumn. I had come home from an academically abysmal but life-enriching educational encounter at the University of Richmond where, that spring semester, I not only sported the only undergraduate beard on campus but also, I rode the only 1932, seventy-four-cubic-inch Harley Davidson with a sidecar in the whole dull town of Richmond.

I was a man of the world or, at least, the U.S. by then. During a year out of college I had journeyed most of the country, mainly by conveyance of thumb, had worked at a railroad yard, and had returned for a final blowout of a semester at the Old U. of R.

Which brings us to the venue of the terrible event of August, 1965. I probably could have gotten my old job back at the railroad but, possibly in avoidance of getting accustomed to great pay and good hard work, instead, I took a job with a construction company for so-so wages and really hard work. I got a job digging holes in the bottom of holes. It was a big project where they had bulldozed a straight-arrow slash through rolling Northern Virginia forest land for a power line right-of-way. At the site where each of the mammoth steel towers was to be erected, a machine had drilled four holes in the ground thirty inches across and ten to fourteen feet deep for concrete footers. My job was to climb down a ladder, which

142

was then removed, and, using shovels and picks with short little handles, dig out the walls into bell-shaped cavities at the bottom of the holes so when they poured the cement it would form a foot at the bottom of the footer and the power towers would never blow down.

After the first day, they paired me up with a kid named Ken who became a friend and who, eventually, drove me out to U.S. Highway 50 at the end of the summer when I headed west for good. But on the first day, after I slid to a dust-cloud stop in front of the contractor's shed and shouted over the *lope-lope-lope* of my motorcycle to the fellow standing there, "Got any jobs?" and after he had shouted back, "Can you dig down in a hole in the ground?" I assured him I was part gopher. Then, after I'd hit a bump and the exhaust system of the Harley had fallen off and the old machine sat dead in the trees next to the rough-rutted road into the project, they hired me and teamed me up with an older Black man whose partner hadn't made it to work that day.

I can't tell you how scared I was going down in a hole the first time. I'd always been a little claustrophobic and from 10 feet down at the bottom of a 30" wide bore, where there was hardly room to sit down, and after the ladder had been pulled up and I knew I was trapped down there, I looked up and the circle of sky above me seemed to be about the size of a quarter. I just sat there with my knees in my face for a few seconds trying to get my composure and decide what to do. I think if the old Harley hadn't broken down and stranded me out there, I might have had the guy up above me with the bucket and rope drop me the ladder and quit on the spot. But, as it was, I was stuck: stuck in the woods and stuck down in the ground. So, I started digging. Tentatively at first and then furiously I went to work, thinking the sooner I'd filled enough buckets with dirt, the sooner I could get out of there and take my turn up in the glorious light, space, and air of daylight pulling the bucket up for the other guy. Then, from above, came the calm, strong voice of a fellow I came to know as Jesse. He said, "Son, jus' because you down in that hole with a shovel don't mean you got to be shovelin' all the time. You got a nice little space cleared out there for yourself, sit down and be glad you in the shade. We be here all summer. We get these damn holes dug."

I filled up the bucket I had been working on so when *The Man* came along Jesse could get busy pulling up a load. Then I took his advice. I sat down and felt the cool earth and realized without panic there was plenty of air down there. Jesse talked to me some more and I knew I could handle it. Later on, during lunch break, he shared a sandwich with me and at quitting time got me a ride back into town with his car pool of Black guys and all of us were dirty and tired and laughing about those damned holes we had been digging in. What a ridiculous job it was and we all knew it.

I came back that evening with a friend and we resuscitated the old motor with baling wire, beer cans, and hose clamps. For the first couple of weeks I rode the bike out to the location each day, rejoicing in the fresh cool morning air of rural roads and scented thickets and the wild freedom of roaring home in the afternoon with the rush of wind upon my sweat-soaked clothes. Then I settled into the sane regularity of riding with Ken and another fellow. I would sit out on the front steps in the morning with my hardhat on and play guitar while waiting for my ride. Sometimes Mom would sit on the couch just inside and listen through the screen door while she smoked a cigarette before starting the morning dishes. On some songs she would sing along with me. Those were such good moments in the summer of my twentieth year while I waited for my ride out to where I dug holes in the bottom of holes.

I even liked the work. After the first few days I got into the rhythm of the job and by the time a month of digging and hauling the dense earth had passed, all the flab of college debauchery had disappeared and I was a lean and powerful young man. Twenty years old and already I had known the danger and adventure of highways while hitching across most of this great country, and had studied matters grand and tedious in the stifle and wonder of the university and now was picking and shoveling in a brotherhood of back-breaking toil as old as the Pyramids.

It seemed that Tommy, the foreman, had a sixth sense for knowing when I was *resting* down in the ground and he would sneak up and drop rocks down to clank on my hard hat. I would jump and then cuss him and with the voice of an ogre growling up from the bowels of the earth threaten to crawl out of the hole and kick his butt. Then we would laugh and sometimes he'd say to be careful down there. That worried me because Tommy wasn't the kind of guy to speak lightly of caution.

I guess, beyond that first day, the next time I was really terrified on the job was when I hit a spring and in moments the dirt and rock became a sucking muck and I had to pull my foot out of one of my boots to free myself and chimney-crawl my way up to daylight. I remember standing up there with one bare foot and all smeared with mud and cursing Ken for being so damned slow getting the ladder. He just stood there looking at me and the aluminum extension ladder he was carrying rattled from the shake of his laughter.

Then as we progressed farther along the right-of-way the geology changed and the dark dirt gave way to rock and, in addition to my pick and shovel, sometimes I had to wrestle with a ninety-pound pneumatic jackhammer. The work was so hard I had to laugh at it down there on my knees cradling the deafening rat-tat-tat jingle of the jackhammer in my arms as I chiseled the granite into bucket-sized chunks for Ken to haul up and, hopefully, not drop on my head.

When you're a twenty-year-old boy/man you can laugh away almost anything that scares you and we did a lot of laughing those days in the rocky holes with granite dust choking us and engine fumes pumping through the compressors that ran the jackhammers. It was another adventure and, besides, most of us were still immortal back then. It was just the old guys like Jesse who knew better, but it was also the old guys who knew you didn't quit steady work when you had a family waiting for the check at the end of every week.

So much of our experience just seems like random pieces of life that are up to us to tie together into a semblance of order, but then there will come moments of intersection when happenstance transcends to profundity. Sometimes it's almost like the elements of a situation are staged for dramatic effect. That's the way it was near quitting time on a late August day when the hole I was working in started coming down on me.

There were probably a dozen of us laborers working in the holes that summer. Each morning we would assemble at the construction shack, and then laden with picks, shovels, buckets, ropes, lunch pails, and water coolers we would climb into a big dump truck and in pairs be dropped off at sites spread out along the dips and ridges of the right-of-way. During the day, as teams would finish one location we would gather our tools and walk up the line to the next set of unfinished holes and start over. Thus each day we progressed a greater distance from the shack and each day meant that the truck ride took longer and the digging time grew shorter. Such was the reward of persistent labor that summer. Every afternoon the truck would head out to the farthest outpost, load that crew, and head back to gather the rest of us. What a fine late-afternoon-hard-day's-work feeling it was to climb up into the truck bed and collapse against the side for an ever-longer ride back.

But this day of choreographed significance we weren't spread out much at all. The whole headquarters of the outfit had been trucked up the line so that all the progress we had made in improving the ratio of toil to travel had been erased. Ken and I had been working in the holes closest to the shack all that day. It was slow going in the rock. The truck made its short run out and was heading back with everybody loaded up—and in the meantime the hole started to fall down on me. Choreographed, you see. Everybody got there and had piled out of the truck, I could hear them talking and shouting up above. It was dry dirt and crumbled rock all moving around me and I was digging frantically with my bare hands trying to free my legs, but the more I moved, the more rock broke loose from the wall. One leg was stuck pretty good and the other was starting to go. Ken was afraid to drop me the ladder because the whole side of the wall was loose and any disturbance might cave it in on me. At first, I wildly tried to dig out but then I got real still because I realized I didn't dare move at all. Tommy was up above then—Tommy and my fellow laborers and the superintendent all there, assembled like the cast of a movie.

I could hear my own breathing, it was so quiet down in that hole. They were talking up above but I was concentrating on my legs and how there still was a little movement left around them but I couldn't risk trying to climb out. It would have brought the whole mess right down on me. And scared. If I hadn't been a twenty-year-old man of the world—a scholar, a traveler, a summer-hardened laborer—I would have been crying for sure. I felt like it then. Crying like a baby just born. Maybe I was just being born that afternoon down in the hole with the crumbling rock and the crumbling of my immortality. Maybe we don't really begin to live until we become thoroughly mortal.

They got a beam across the top of the hole and then they lowered the heavy rubber hose from the air compressor. Tommy said to get ahold of it and I grabbed it with my rock-bloodied hands and gripped it with all my life. They started pulling me up—Tommy, Ken, and God knows how many others up there pulling me toward the twenty-five cents worth of sky so far above me. Suspended by the hose, I worked my legs free and they pulled me out.

I was too damned scared to hide it or care either, shaking and likely pale of face. But I had handled it right. I hadn't cried or pleaded or prayed, at least out loud. There was some laughing and looking away, but no one there would have made a better showing and they all knew it.

I didn't laugh or look away at all. I just stood back at a safe distance glaring at the hole and at the cloud of dust rising out of it as it completely collapsed.

Tommy was looking down at the rubble.

Jesse had stepped away from where he had helped haul me up out of the earth.

Jesse was gathering timbers.

Tommy looked over at me.

How could I ever go down into that hole again?

He saw my question and in a voice that carried to me and beyond to all who were there and beyond that to the whole world, without a trace of malice he said, 'Don't worry, Nichols. You won't have to go back down there. We'll shore it up with timbers and I'll put a Nigger in the hole tomorrow."

And in that simple statement all the injustice of the world was spoken. In that gravest insult I had ever heard uttered, that devastatingly demeaning pronouncement of the lesser humanity of all the people of color with whom I shared this blessed Earth, that direct and unthinking damnation more cruel and cutting than the backs of busses, the "Colored" outhouses behind filling stations, the "separate but equal" hypocrisy of post-slavery America, was, also, the telling of my own shallow truth about principle versus survival.

In a voice not even spoken, only thought, that no one heard except me, and I hear it now—I mean, I had marched for "jobs and freedom" with Dr. Martin Luther King, I had sung with the voice of 200,000 at the Lincoln Memorial, "We shall overcome... " I had shared an egg-salad sandwich with Jesse and called him my friend—in absolute, cold-silent terror I said, "Yeah, Tommy, put him in the hole."

Author's Note

It's been a long time since the summer of 1965 when I was a kid digging "holes in the bottom of holes" back in Virginia.

Years.

The Civil Rights Movement in America was still a bloody battle back then. I mean, Martin Luther King was still alive. There was a long way to go.

There still is.

You see, the enforced expectations of *political correctness* mean nothing if they only give manners to madness. How courteous we are these days. Why, we wouldn't think of using the 'N' word in public. Would we? Regardless of whether or not *Nigger* is still in the vernacular of our hearts.

I wonder about Tommy, the foreman by whom those bitterly ugly words were so easily spoken. I'll wager he would be a bit more careful in his choice of words today as he indifferently sent another Black man down into a treacherous hole.

And, of course, I wonder about myself, the White kid who was so frightened by the intensity of the situation that those bitter ugly words made perfectly good sense. I'm not certain, but I still don't think my compliance was so much a matter of racism as self-survival. In the immediate moments after my rescue from that miserable hole, if Tommy had said, "Don't worry, Nichols—we'll shore it up and send your *mother* down tomorrow," I just might have gone along with the idea. I honestly don't know. But the most troubling part of my recollection of that terrible day is not what Tommy said or what I didn't say. It's the fact that, before anything was said at all, the situation was obvious to Jesse. Such was the soul-deep poison of racism that was the reality of his world.

Jesse was gathering timbers. Now that is a wrong that will take more than the force of law, the deception of manners, and a few decades of *equal opportunity* to fix.

R. Nichols
(2015)

True Times
(1968)

He had been murdered the day before and no one really said much about it. Especially the Black people didn't have anything to say to me. There were more of them than us at the factory—maybe seventy-five percent Black and it was in '68 when violence was always possible.

Spring 1968, and some bastard had killed Martin Luther King at the garbage strike down in Memphis. The electricians and the other White men in the maintenance department mumbled at each other when I got to work that morning and then, knowing my beliefs, glanced around and almost in harmony said to me, "So your boy's dead, huh?"

"Yeah," I said.

Then the factory started up. Giant flywheels turned. The huge machines punched and roared and sparked. Shears and punch presses and lathes and grinders and drill presses growled and hissed—the vast building filled with noise. I became lost in the massive project of stamping and cutting and burning and drilling the hard shapes into parts, and parts into moving, strong, and functioning machines to be loaded on trucks and set off to customers who made greater things of our small products: our air compressors to fill the tires, paint the fenders, run the pavement-striking jackhammers.

It was very loud but still I could tell, the Blacks weren't talking. I asked John, a Black guy my age who worked with me most days, and he said it was too bad King had died and nothing more.

Then they turned the factory off.

Ten o'clock.

Some master switch was pulled. The great wheels were shut down. They clicked for moments while they slowed and slowed and finally stopped. There was a PA system that usually couldn't be heard, but this time we listened.

"We will observe a five-minute period of silence in memory of Dr. Martin Luther King."

150

Silence, that kind of silence, the kind following dense noise, it has a feel—an actual tactile presence prickled at me.

The electricians and the other White maintenance men walked to the repair shop and poured coffee from their thermoses.

Silence. I was alone—sitting on a stack of pallets. Everyone except the White maintenance men who, of course, were too aloof to show it, seemed stunned. Work had never quit like that before.

I heard them laughing—the maintenance men and electricians sitting with their feet up drinking coffee and laughing while we sat in deep quiet for a great man. They didn't even look around to see who was listening. They just laughed. It was nothing. Nothing. Clear across the factory, their laughter.

They were wrong—something had happened.

It wasn't obvious but it was real. The factory roared again and people worked and I continued searching eyes for reactions while I lifted and shoved and stacked.

Weeks later, the White guys were still laughing and saying how it served the damned Nigger right. And the Black guys still didn't say much about it.

The office was filled with White people and somewhere amid the metal filing cabinets and the tidy desks there was the White voice that had given the order for the five-minute shutdown.

They knew it. I knew it. Maybe even the electricians, in their own malicious and defensive ways, knew too. We knew how frightened we were of dead Dr. King and his seemingly apathetic dark mass that had scared the factory silent for five good minutes.

That's power.

Casual Jokes of Hatred
(1999)

I work with a man who is so embittered by life that he casually jokes about the death of "Nigger children."

I fear for the children, all the children of all the diverse colors and languages and cultures. I know this man's virulent racial hatred is not some freakish aberration of a single life of sorrow, loss, and self-pity. It is epidemic among the ignorant throughout this world.

Bless the babies, may they know the Love that is resplendent in this garden crystallized from void and vastness, this Earth, this community of life.

And—though, personally, I'll have to leave it up to more compassionate folks like, say, Jesus and the Buddha—bless this loathing fool. May he glean from the vision of an unguarded moment, the Love that is ambient in the much grander universe of which he is unknowingly an integral part.

If there is any consolation here, this hate-poisoned victim of his own wrath is one of the most miserable bastards I've ever had the misfortune of knowing.

One way or another, racism sure brings out the worst in all of us.

Slumber Station

There's a train in the storm,
I heard it rumbling through the night—
its headlight spiking lightning
through the gloom.

With its cattle-car cargo
of hell-bound souls,
and its wind-howling whistle
shrieking doom.

**2017 Update on
Racism**

Inauguration Day
January 20, 2017

Damn.

A Path to the City
R. Nichols / 2000/2017

PART IV

Other Views from the Path
People, Sketches,
Situations Suspended in Poem

The path of the observer need not be one of highways and distant isles. It is the step of each mundane day and the quirks and wonders, the terrors and miracles experienced as we pass.

The character of a nation. The formative experiences of life's major adventures. The exotic milestones and wonders of our way.

But sometimes... most of the time, actually, our paths are colored by the stark, sweet, and just startlingly ordinary observations of events and people we encounter on the journey from there to here.

I'll describe a touch of what I have discovered. Some of this is really sad. Some will save you from despair; some might give you a hit of the bleak. I tell the scenes, the vignettes in this collection as a poet living a real life and sharing it with you. Your eyes have been open, your hearts attuned and, thus, you know that such vulnerability is the essence of compassion.

Paths

Paths:
each new day presents Frost's options—
paths to be taken... or not
And each successive morning—
a portion of their cure.

Just a Traveler

…just a traveler
in the moment of red-signal lights
streaking past the window of this all-night train.

I lived beside a rushing Rocky Mountain stream
where waters passed in transition
from trickle of melting snow toward raging might
of the earth-wrapping seas.
Those waters moved in diamond sunlight sparkle
and swirling subtle eddies
against the stone moments of
mountains,

passing like this midnight
train through Indiana.

Days upon the Highway (highway song)

Days upon the highway,
nights beside a road—
make me sit
and wonder why.

Then there're mornings
full of sunshine,
evenings by a stream,
and stars a-spinning
mysteries in the sky.

I'm not saying this life
is the right way.
Wouldn't recommend it
to a friend or foe.
But for me I know
it's the best way—
yes, the highway
is the life I need to know.

You can view me singing this song on the side of Old Highway
66. Go to Youtube.com and search for: Road Song / Old Route
66. Or you can tediously type in the address—

https://www.youtube.com/watch?v=-IXPzpDZXx8

159

The Street-Man

The street-man called to me. I ignored him for a couple of steps. It was easy. I was past his face and could have easily escaped his pathetic need. But then I turned back.

"The man stops to talk with me," he said, speaking his thoughts aloud.

"What's going on?" I asked, knowing exactly what was going on.

"Just…some change," he said, and his words were broken by alcohol and he was disoriented by my turn. Most, I'm sure, and for their own good reasons, keep walking and dismiss his discomfiting existence from their own safe realms.

I gave him five quarters.

He didn't say thank you. He just mumbled something about hard times and I lied and said I understood. Then he focused his booze-blurred eyes deeply into mine and said, "I'm doing my best."

As I walked away, he stood there staring vacantly, still holding out his hand with my coins in it and repeated, "I'm doing my best."

"Yeah, you are," I said, speaking my thoughts aloud. "But, am I?"

A Sad Little Girl

They brought a sad little girl into the restaurant this morning. She had undergone some kind of surgery and much of her body was wrapped in a stiff cast. They rolled her in on a modified wheelchair, propped her up, and while her mother and friends talked about aerobics classes, as an aside, they fed her juice and oatmeal. She was a symbol of her mother's courage and, hence was chided several times when the glint of small-child tears erupted silently from the corners of her eyes.

Sweet Scene on a Downtown Sidewalk

And,
his rumbling motorcycle silenced,
he crouches.

His leather weapons belt,
his short-waisted-leather jacket.

His official blue police helmet
sits upon the seat.

His severe military haircut.

But his ridged demeanor
softens as he kneels
before the department-issue-tool kit
spread upon the sidewalk before him.
He adjusts the brake mechanism
of the malfunctioning electric wheelchair
whose passenger,
in thrashing moans of motion,
had communicated
his need.

Try that,
gestures the stoic lawman.

And,
in nonverbal poem of the body spirit,
the wheelchair man
turns two sidewalk circles, and,
with joy oblivious to

163

the contortion that imprisoned him,
speeds off—

liberated.

The night-stick man.
The 9mm man.
The motorcycle man
slips a smile.
Having accomplished
the best deed
of his day,
he rides off

to ticket jay walkers
and hassle winos.

Scene from the City

The tattered lady
was heaped up in a fetal ball
beneath a filthy blanket
on the damned sidewalk,
sleeping in a downtown doorway.

Cold night.
It was bitter December cold.
The town, festive with the season.
Sidewalks crowded—
gaudy floats, giant balloons, marching bands
had passed—
they called it "The Parade of Lights."
Giddy shivering folks scattered.

She was down on the cement,
shadowed from the street ights—
having dreams
while the rest of the world
chatted and shook
and waited for a bus
to take them home.

Silhouette-Man Passing

Silhouette to the passing cars, his image moved across the South Broadway storefronts like an unclaimed soul.

The joints were no good anymore. The knees would not bend so he had to move the old bike by stiffly stepping upon the sidewalk the way children ride their first bicycles before they have the balance to pedal.

He had never killed, though, surely, he had stolen and lied. But he had never hurt the children.

Though the night was clearly not his friend, it was his only time. Days were cluttered with strong legs and purposes and there was no place for him. Nights were an empty space in which to move about and seek the death that had neglected him. Even the wine had quit being his friend.

Steadily he moved along the sidewalk through the night's heatless neon glare.

In front of the Center for the Aged, there was a large car and an impatient daughter with dark hair and no kindness. And there were four old ladies all wearing light-colored raincoats who, with their white hair and their white faces and their stalling progress toward the open car doors in the dim light, could have been marble statues forever implanted in the cement sidewalk. They didn't move as he rolled past them with labored air and the bearded visage of an abandoned life.

As he moved on beneath the viaduct, cars drifted off Broadway and up the ramp toward the interstate where their taillights rushed into the interminable line of motion toward disappearing distances— like points of memory irretrievably swept from consciousness.

Beggar-Man and the Blessing of the Child

He had crawled out from under some miserable Platte River bridge, scruffily-clothed and filthy; distraught with the booze and insanity; dazed by the cacophony of demons mumbling through his mind. He shivered. His cardboard sign was a scrawled rant of a plea for the *homeless-hungry-anything-helps-God-bless-thank-you* dollars of light-paused morning commuters.

She wore a pretty pink and puffy winter coat—so tiny out there on the sidewalk walking toward the tattered hulk of the beggar— maybe four-years old, tentative but not afraid. Her dad stood guard as he sent his precious child upon a mission of mercy, armed with pure heart and a coin.

On the ceiling of the Sistine Chapel, Michelangelo painted the reach of God to the outstretched need of humanity.

I saw the wild-eyed street man soften as he reached toward the small child's gift. I saw the little girl as she blessed the beggar with her smile.

For an instant, perhaps, his soul was safe from torment and fear and rage.

Captive at a Fast Food Café

The man who busses tables here,
a Latino with a thick black mustache
and a face of serious mahogany,
glanced at me with resignation—
captive at a fast food café.

Oasis Beside the Rolling Road

Road café.
Oasis beside the rolling road,
haven from the blowing corn,
respite from the crucifix utility poles
in regimented progression
toward the infinite focus of all straight lines.

As the waitress picks and spreads crushed ice
across the bottom of the salad-bar cart,
it is 9:43 a.m. on an early October morning
in Norfolk, Nebraska,
and difficult not to despair
for the momentum of my species.

But…
I think I'll write a poem for the waitress.

To the Waitress in the Red Sweater

As one who likely will never
pause in this town again,
and who, with the anonymity of assured distance
to protect you from the threat of his honesty,
can write from an uninhibited heart—

I'll tell you, waitress in the red sweater,
as I watched you spreading ice in the bottom
of the salad-bar cart,
and, absorbed the closeness of your being as you
refilled my coffee cup,

and heard you say to the threesome who wished
to order biscuits and gravy,
"I'll have to go count the biscuits,"

it occurred to me
that you are beautiful.

October 23, 1988 / South of Norfolk, Nebraska / Club 8

The Old Boys

The old boys are gathered—n ne, maybe ten of them—about a large table and, clutching coffee cups they talk trucks and football.

Down here in Texas, colleges participate in a high school draft for the best players—serious business.

It's snowing this morning. A wet-sloppy inch of a mess to make the red mud thick and slick.

They've got plenty to talk about, these gray-haired, red-and-cracked-faced farmers, these merchants, these local home lads never gone long from the county. So, it is a mix of gridiron picks and pickup trucks—a jostle of Ford vs. Chevrolet discourse.

"So, Doc. Who pushed that Ford of yours out the driveway this blizzardy mornin'?"

"Don't you worry none about my Ford, Teddy. What I want to know is who lent you the jumper cables to start that Chevy of yours to rattlin'?"

Some, seated across the café, glancing over the tops of their reading glasses, would scoff and call it small talk and then return to their morning papers.

I would call it an embrace.

February 5, 1998
Vernon, Texas / La Casa Mia Café / 8:49 a.m.

Finish

The sun glanced back with
warm breath—
yellow-orange dust clouds drifted
behind the
rumble-steady tractor.

Then, day-tired,
the farmer squinted
up horizon-touching rows
at the empty sky and,
seeing no sun
and feeling the blue-arc
world-edge closing,
stilled the machine
and left on dusty feet—
while gray-chilled dirt clouds settled
day death upon the field.

Denver Bus Terminal at Two A.M.

Two a.m. at the Denver Bus Terminal. Fifty or sixty people in various postures of discomfort and anxiety sat and paced about on the hard floor. There is something in a city that, once it holds you for a short time, so often maims—causes one to limp, to have twisted limbs and stalking eyes, perverse, possessed. And there is something in a downtown bus terminal that grotesquely clarifies the city's atrocities. Women with flawless and cream-like complexion merely step into the blue glare of the terminal and immediately develop hideous flaws and irregular blotches upon their faces. Fathers with beloved wives and children in long-distant homes enter this denuding realm and—with wino's gait and degenerate mask—wander here leering at the travel-eroded masses of men, women, and children.

Once a man followed me into the restroom of a bus terminal and stared intently at my organ commenting about how much he like the small suitcase which I held at arm's length at my side. "It isn't all that small," I said as I briskly exited.

I'll tell you about bus terminals. They can be outposts of a dangerous frontier of city evil. Or havens, warm places against the frigid steel and glass and threat of the streets. They are twenty-four-hour food and light. But, just as a well-seasoned yet untidy kitchen is a haven for cockroaches, the bus terminal is a nesting ground for the creatures of dark streets.

Most anytime of the day there is a malaise, an inflicted apathy and discomfort that infects the transient masses at bus terminals. There is the essence of a hopelessness, a sense of mortal oppression manifest in the milling figures of humanity dimly illuminated by the purplish chill of neon and beckoned by the near-incomprehensible recitation of destinations and gate numbers as they stand in listless lines. Blood-drained travelers tenaciously heading nowhere.

There are drunks, of course, and drug addicts and prostitutes and soul-vacant street people seeking respite from the harshness of the sidewalks. They are the resident populations who furtively seek shelter by shifting about among the dismal crowds in avoidance of the scrutiny of authority. In trembling stench, wild-eyed and dangerous, shivering in scant skirts and the false radiance of rouge and clown-sad painted smiles, bundled in layers of neglect; they are society's embarrassment—its alcoholic uncle, its bad son and wayward daughter, the lost ones. But we must abide their lurking presence for we know them to be as close to ourselves as are poverty and insanity and fear. It is not their plight about which I write.

I'll tell of the travelers awaiting the busses.

There are miserable children sprawled upon the spit-filthy floor, lost to the rigors of fitful sleep and confusion and clinging to the frazzled forms of motherhood. Bearing the burden of innumerable suitcases and draped by shopping bags stuffed with snacks and games and cans of pop, mothers scold their scattering hordes while balancing upon a jutting hip the stained and startled clasp of an infant—somewhere in the deluge of possession and temporal distraction there is always a cache of new and not so new diapers. The mothers and their children. Where are the fathers?

The old people are so often in a dazed state, in constant need of reassurance from the impatient ticket agents and baggage handlers, repeatedly inquiring of others in their queue, "Is this the line for the Las Vegas bus?" They are never certain of the status of their luggage or the location of their tickets and they check and re-check pockets and purses. And, as with so much of the inelegance of aged demeanor, they are equally uncertain if they have sufficient stamina to survive the battering challenge of overland travel.

It seems that 90% of the people have already traveled for three-and-a-half days and still have another forty or so hours to go before they reach their journey's end. It adds new dimensions to the expanse of this great country when traversed by motor coach.

And, amidst this plebeian ménage, there is always a contingent of passengers who, being neither old nor maternally encumbered, feel the necessity of announcing to anyone who will listen and all within earshot that normally they take the plane.

Everyone is so worn and weary, even the rare passengers who are just beginning their trek. Such persons, glowing in the essence of health and energy, are let off at the front door, hugged farewell by loved ones, blessed by "bon voyage," and then just as they jauntily scoop up their luggage and swing through the bus station

174

door are instantly afflicted by the 'terminal curse" and transformed into pallid and soulless wanderers of a lethargic realm.

So it is that we masses of pale and pimpled, frail and tangled, bodily bruised and spiritually deflated assemble for the diverse purposes of budget travel.

With the exception of local and remote destinations where other forms of mass transportation are unavailable, those who choose to endure the arduous trials of mass transit upon the highways and in the bus stations of this nation are often the self-effacing victims of a false and martyrized sense of economy, whether by tradition of desperation, ignorance, or the intimidation of image; it seems that many overlook the possibility of airine transport as a consideration in their perception of travel. In fact, there are often situations of distance, time, and resource which can prove a four-hour transcontinental flight to be less expensive than a four-day sojourn in the meandering hell of all-night busses and the pimp-and-pusher-infested dens of bus terminals.

Perhaps such a prevalence of misery that is the contagion of the terminal is not primarily the product of road fatigue, the ingestion of rest-stop ptomaine, or the aggravation of incessant delay. Could it not be that this pall of desperation is the inherent condition of the downtrodden that lies in remission within most of us until nurtured by bitter circumstance—the bus terminal becoming a microcosm for a world of greater struggle?

Despair goes traveling and it takes us all along for the ride.

I Saw the Clipping

I saw the clipping
cut from some insignificant
corner of the *Post*.
It had yellowed—
already ancient news
by the time I read it.

I guess it's true that
Georgie Becker was bludgeoned to death—
found broken and smashed in a skid-row alley.

He was never really a childhood friend.
Too weird, too twisted to be a friend...
he was just a kid who was always around.
A kid who would take any of our filthy dares
just to always be around, I suppose,
and to make us feel sick for our spittle
upon his marshmallow,
and to make us cringe at the memory of the bleak white
flesh of his buttocks bared to the parading
disgust of school children.

(Nobody was supposed to take such dares
and make us all perverse.)

They found him there,
a male Caucasian in his thirties;
not just dead
but crusted in dare-desperate blood
and pathetically twisted in disjointed supplication
beneath the alley rubble.

I heard it nearly ki led his mother,
Mrs. Becker up the street.

A Visit Downtown

The wild-man of a staggering drunk
who grasped my arm and sang
some rowdy old song
as we skipped through downtown
Saturday shoppers 'til
parting at the corner
with, "Take it easy."

The ever-eyed girl who sat
in the wooden-seated bus station
delicately sketching the harsh-lit scene—
the worn-thin people, the
frozen edge of the moment;
and how she blushed at my notice
of her masterwork,
shyly closing her thick spiral notebook.

Where to my sunny cool afternoon,
where to?

Just a visitor, you know.
I walked to my car
and as I started to pull away,
pleading, a desperate man
with a tap on the window—
which way to the YMCA?

Old Man and the Twisted Metal

The old man had a voice like ash and eyes that glared with ragged-edged rage.

We were ten years old. My buddy Melvin and I had collected a stack of scrap metal from the gas company dump and, instead of hauling it back home with us, had decided that we would just go down in the woods and throw what we had onto the old man's pile.

We didn't know him, but we knew where he camped.

With a crash, we tossed our cache of twisted metal on his heap and it became indistinguishable in the rubble of his camp. With a quickness that totally surprised us, he leaped from the woods and had both of us by the arms—grasping us with a terrible grip.

"I'll turn you both to scrap, you goddamned thieves. I'll kill you dead for stealing a man's metal. Dead I say!"

It nearly always catches me off guard when someone starts crying. It might have been both of us, I don't know. I just know it was hard to speak.

I was a kid and I was scared but, even then, I knew some things can't be said.

Melvin choked out, "No, mister. We aren't stealing. We brought you some stuff."

He let go but there was fierceness in his voice. "Just get the hell away from me. Goddamn you. Leave my metal alone!"

What I had wanted to say was that it was a gift.

But, I don't think he could have understood that. Too mad, too ruined, too much like the jagged scrap pile himself to ever accept a gift.

Melvin and I ran clear out of the woods—shaken and glad to be alive.

"Well shit," said Melvin.

"Yeah," I said.

Sam

Sam was a dancer,
and his wild-flung arms and blurred motions
filled the whole room,
and his presence dominated
the smoke-filled blotches of colored light
vaguely defining the size and character of the place.

And the woman,
in shining, skin-tight, breast-filled and rounded-ass
costume,
would mimic and shadow his magnificent gyrations.
She was sex. And when she moved—slow and looking at
him
like he was something that tasted good—her whole body
was
one unified, magnetic, hungry, clenching copulatory
swallow.

Sweat and booming base guitar, smell of bourbon and
sounds of woman-man laughter-shrieking and the blur
of Sam and the slow tease of his woman:
night-scene through the crystals of an ice cube—
sensations and smoke.

And Sam was a strange man, dangerously filled with
vibrations of his own being, and dangerously close to
shattering the minds of those who filled the shadows
between the colored spotlights under which he performed.

Sam was a slashing figure with flashing teeth that
smiled snarling dares, and with shoes that mirrored in
black
the whirling lights and energy,
he was a dangerous man.

I watched him with awe and curiosity and laughter and
a tinge of dark hatred—
he was such a swirling enigma of a man,
with his deceitful smile and his flashy two-bit clothes…

And now, from my dark end of the bar,
with him turning in maniac contortions,
boiling and effervescing throughout the room…
I know—
somebody's going to kill him someday.

It's an All-Cowboy Music Night

It's an all-cowboy music night
and only a scatter of cowboys at the bar.
It's Western Colorado on a clear, cold
October evening.
Another big hat and pointy-toed boots
just came in.
Wintery winds broke through
the front door with him,
asking a question
no one wanted to answer,

And the bartender,
such a gem he was,
just told his wife,
the waitress,
to quit bullshitting with the customers
and get to work.
And clever, too, he was.
He asked, "Are your ears cold?
Is that why you've got
your head up your ass?"

What delight
the highway holds this night.
It's all part of the town joke:
horseless cowboys and maudlin
honkytonk love songs.

We all know it's starting to snow.

I don't say a damned thing.
I know words
can be a peril to a stranger.

Besides,
I am only a visitor
here,
and about to vamoose
(as the cowboys put it).

Gathering,
I start to rise from my table.
The waitress, wife-of-the-jerk,
puts a soft hand upon my shoulder
and says,
"Sure you don't want another beer, Hon?"

I glance over, seeing the angry eyes
of the barkeep,
and then, honest to God,
I bless her with my smile—
and without risk of words,
silently tell her she is beautiful.

I only say,
"No thanks, Love.
I'm going to try and
get ahead of this storm."

He Might Have Been Joking

He might have been joking when he threatened to hit his wife, but, nonetheless, she cringed.

7:30 p.m. / Charleston, West Virginia / TGI Friday

'Merican Eatin' Dinner
R. Nichols

Inclusion

The young lady with the broom moved about the restaurant gathering scraps and wiping off tabletops. She was invisible to most. Just another slow person in a fast world.

The teenaged girls were so beautiful and full of life. Their light laughter lilted through the Arby's.

Those lovely girls, so blessed—I worried as the lobby girl approached them. Sometimes the most fortunate can be the most cruel.

But these cheerleaders, both of them—their beauty was not just so shallow as flowing locks and songbird voices. They stopped their chatter and brought the girl into their world with words that made her smile and together the three laughed in some connection of teenaged culture.

That touched me.

It can be so dangerous out there for slow people in a fast world.

Over the years, I have left people poems. I dropped these words off on their table and left.

To the Two Girls in the Next Booth

I noticed your interactions
with the sweeping girl.
Such compassion—
such honest and open discovery
of the common bonds
of humanity
that transcend affl ction.

Bless you both.

Washer-Man

By the stench of the porch he knew that she would not pay. The work was hardly worth doing when they didn't pay—his commission was only paid on cash repairs and sales, and the meager hourly wage was a weak token for the labor and skill involved.

The porch smelled of spoiled things. His experienced eyes carefully avoided searching through the stacks of rubble cluttering the planks for the organic source of the odor.

When he had started the job a year earlier, he was disgusted by the greed of the other repairmen. They would pressure people for cash, or, better, to sell them new appliances whether needed or not. Then the boss had put him on commission, too, and he had seen, in steady and bitter acquiescence, the crumpling of his lofty ideals.

When they were old and their houses were sloppy they never paid.

She walked ahead of him through the kitchen toward a side porch. "The washer's out here. Never mind those dishes. I'm going to wash them today." There were dozens and dozens of dishes stacked on every surface of the dim kitchen. He saw the dried food and the mold and sensed the cockroaches apathetically staring at him from the kitchen table.

She wore a flowered robe. It was faded and torn at several of the seams. Her hair was many colors of gray and brown. Her face was shallow. On the wall of the kitchen was a cardboard print of an old man praying over a few crumbs of bread.

"It just popped and burnt out a fuse. The water had backed up from the drain and the tub spilled over and then it just popped right back there." She was pointing to the rear of the old machine. "I smelled electricity and was afraid to try it again."

"It will be a hundred dollars if it needs a new motor. The machine is over twenty-years old—hardly worth fixing. Perhaps it's only a burnt wire, I'll check." He lifted a side of the washer and turned it from the wall. It was quite heavy because it was full of water that had stood for a week in the tub and had stagnated.

There were thirteen hex-headed screws—each one caked with twenty years of untended filth. The lady said nothing as he removed the back panel. He blew away the dust from the terminals on the motor and one by one he traced each wire to the timer, to the various switches, and then he traced the wires back again to the motor. He wanted to find a broken wire so that he could quickly fix it and then be gone before too many of the surfaces of the house had touched his Monday morning clothes and his Monday morning flesh.

"I'm afraid the wires are all fine, it must be your motor."

"Oh, God, not the motor," she whispered.

"Well, I'll hook it back up and try it. Maybe I'll find something simpler, cheaper." He grabbed the cord from where it had fallen in the mouse dung behind the washer. He plugged it into the ancient socket half way up the wall of the porch. He hoped that the machine would work so that he could get on to the clean, middle-aged customers who paid with rich green cash or with checks printed on pastel mountain scenes, or ocean lighthouses scenes.

"Here goes, Ma'am, I hope it works." And he pulled the switch on the face of the timer and with a slush of movement the rancid water began to turn with the spinning of the old tub and with the sucking of the resurrected pump, the level of water lowered through the black drain hose and out through the now-open drain.

The old lady said, "Praise the Lord, I knew He could do it."

"Yeah, the water must have dried out of the motor and apparently didn't do any real damage."

"I prayed and He heard me. My loving personal savior heard me and made my washer all right. I only owe you the fifteen dollars for coming, right?" You didn't fix anything, did you? I just have to pay you for coming here. On the phone they said that fifteen dollars—fourteen ninety-five—that would be what it cost to get you to come. That's all I have to pay, isn't it? The Lord fixed it, didn't He?"

"Sure, Ma'am, God fixed your washer, I won't charge you for something I didn't fix." And he thought of how the Lord must have also been the one who clogged up her damned sewer in the first place.

And then, in a rhythm he had heard from others and with words that had been spoken to him by rote many times before, she invited him to accept the Lord Jesus Christ to be his personal savior and when he said no thanks she proceeded to tell him of his fate while he replaced the thirteen miserable screws. She told him that he would be thrown into the depths of hell and there his flesh would burn in non-consumptive screaming agony for eternity.

"That's fourteen ninety-five."

I'll pay that in four payments starting next month."

"That's fine, just sign here."

"I'll pray for you."

"Thank you, goodbye."

He stepped outside into the dull chill of late November and glanced about at the rubble of fallen leaves strewn from the careless trees by the discordant wind. And, looking up at the gray face of the sky, he thought of how, just like the old lady, this day wasn't going to pay.

I awoke one morning and this story, though fictional, seemed so real I don't think I've ever really gotten over it. This is the only work of fiction included in this book.

Oh, My Goodness

You've got to know this, Ann. Sometimes you don't know the whole picture and it can all seem so hopeless.

It was just for a moment this afternoon at the damned rest home. Out on the sun porch. Dave was sitting at the table trying to think of something funny to say to our lifelong buddy, Frank, who like normal these days, seemed empty, erased. We could see Tom coming in across the parking lot. You had gone for the iced tea and were coming out the door with a tray. I just stood there next to Frank. Pretty much silent, you know.

What can you say?

Frank was, like usual, standing straight and tall and lean but his eyes were squinted. Confused.

Then the miracle happened.

Ann, you've got to know this.

Frank turned to me and his face came back from the terrible distances for only that moment and he said, "Old Tom's parked his pickup, Dave's leaning back in his chair. You guys..."

And the screen door swung open as you pushed through. A smile broke his face for a split instant and he said, "And, oh, my goodness, here comes my Annie."

Girl Playing in the Ocean

I'll never forget, on a vacation up in Oregon in the cool of early spring, watching the sea from our deck. The lovely girl in a bikini running into the surf—I mean it was fifty degrees and the Pacific waters are always cold and the waves were gray and the surf curled white spray beneath the great clouds that reached from the horizon clear to the steep, green, misty mountains—and her husband just standing there on the sand shivering as she shrieked some taunting jeer over her bare shoulder and dived on in beneath the gray-black wall of an 8' wave and, in youth and fearless lust, was gone to the exhilarating roll of the Ocean.

And I searched the waters with binoculars and he stood weakly on the safe sands and the great sea churned and the surf lay down upon the shore. She emerged with a trilling song of thrill and chill that reached my distant hearing and she stood there in the knee-deep draw of returning waters all a-roil about her legs, and the blessed wave had washed the top of her suit down about her waist and, with bare breasts and nipples erect in the frigid turn of wind, she laughed with such delight as she stretched the modesty of cloth back across the glorious rise of her flesh.

He turned away in disgust.

Her laughing fell away like the falling call of some sad sea bird.

I'll never be the same.

Red Sneakers

There are so many ways to be sad.
Yesterday I was sad about an old lady
who was our waitress at a small-town café,
out where we like to catch lunch while
trucking about the Eastern Colorado oil patch.
Just some farmers and some truckers we were…
And I was sad
because she wore nice little red sneakers
and I knew that she would be dead.

Just like that, I knew.

But, you know…
she had almost a skip to her movement
about the place.
And, my God,
the plates of pork chops and potatoes
she brought out for us,
and the way she lit up
when she said,
"Eat up, Boys!"

Well,
sad, sure,
but…
this day we live.
It's a real gift.

A Dark Little Baby

A dark little baby in a white, white sunsuit
runs with round little feet
to keep up with Daddy
as he cuts the apartment
grass-strip between the sidewalk and the street
while Mama laughs and mock-jogs ten feet behind—
how good they have it this day.

Just a bit of historical perspective.

The Farmer

In the time of Hannibal
there lived an historic non-entity,
an alpine farmer
who gained great renown among
other alpine non-entities—
a great grower
who fertilized his bloodless fields of grain
with elephant dung.

The Factory Ladies' Reunion

It was a year ago when they had been laid off and scattered by the cold whims of commerce—a year since the factory shut down. And now, on this wintery morning they gathered at the long table at the Iron Skillet Restaurant out by the interstate highway. First it was just three of them who wondered nervously if they were to be the whole party. Then more came, and more—mostly alone, some in pairs, wearing nice clothes, slacks and blouses and with touches of jewelry and makeup, careful hair, they wanted to look nice— hesitating at the entryway, each searching the room, and then discovering familiar faces at the long table in the back. They smiled and came on in until the table was filled with friends and the room astir with their warm greetings and excited talk.

The assembled factory ladies all had found new jobs: one sews clothes, another peddles perfumes and soaps, one assembles, several mix and sort. All were worse off than when the good times were in full swing at the factory and there was plenty of overtime and no talk of it ever ending. But, after a rough year, they all were working, getting by.

"… God I miss you girls…" said one with a sigh and then a light laugh to pass it off as just another lesson in "such is life."

But, not everyone had shown up. Several of the gang—the old day shift from a corner of the defunct factory that had melded each of their good years of toil together—some of the girls were not there. Little was said—for the gaiety of the morning, as they all knew (almost as they knew any other superstition) was a fickle gift, easily nixed by the chilled truths about life, *such as it is.* They knew some of their friends were still on the outside seeking their ways—not ready for inclusion in this celebration of survival.

How in louder and faster voices they told each of their long year's journeys to this morning.

How, in blurs of word and gesture, they gave account in short moments of the turning of months.

It would never be the same.

"… no kidding, Loraine," she said, "not a day went by we didn't get the current episode…every day… I used to know more about your kids than I did my own."

It would never be the same.

"…we can't let another year go without getting together…"

The breakfast dishes were pushed back, coffee cups were down to the final bitter sip, and, with embraces and laughter and near-teared farewells, they left.

How awful it must have been a year ago when it all went down.

I Caught the Glance

There.
I caught the glance
and smile of the
gray-haired lady
as she left the café.

Strong kind eyes
heeding my wordless greeting.

Damn.
How she hated the oxygen
tank she dragged behind—
but, oh how she did love those
decades of the cigarette.

Regret and wisdom
were vibrant
in her smile.

Whispered

This is the way it could be—
life is...
a terrible answer
to a terrible question.
I have sensed it so often.
Sometimes I know
a taste of its poison
myself.

It is whispered.

(The old lady's eyes were empty.
I saw her there across the way
nursing a cup of coffee.
And she wasn't just tired.
No, she was finished.
I heard it in her sigh.)

It is bolt-sudden from the silent soul.

(And with his back arcing grotesquely
like a rainbow,
the dead man,
twisted and violently spent
lay upon the pavement—
silhouetted by the glaring
headlights.)

And known by the harsh
mumbled tell of mundane truth...

This message that curses
all who know no more
than a day's pay,

no more than a heated room,
a microwave dinner,
the time-bludgeoned
indifference of
a habitual lover.
(And when his desk was cleared
and his last timecard clocked,
and his days became just
the pacing of
a narrow hallway of some
Arizona-Senior-Sunshine
Trailer-land tin can...)

To each of our days,
this is the awful question
that whisper-shouts
its weary doom:

Why the hell bother?

Whew.
Yes, it could just be this way—
the grand total of the worth
of our days—
disheartened resignation,
stark mortality,
fruitless toil and hollow reward.

Yeah, *why bother.*

But, Hey!
If I can't come up with
something better
than stanzas of
null-set groveling
into uselessness,
then this poet
should cease his song
and mute such artful
utterance of misery.

Okay.
Let me tell you
why life is worth the breath and blood
astir within—
no kidding,
if it isn't this simple,
then it isn't real
and none of us have a chance.

Today I had the best
Egg McMuffin of my life.
I've eaten easily
a billion of the damned things,
but today—wow.
The best Canadian bacon, egg, American cheese,
English muffin meal of all.
And just as I write these words
in celebration of life itself,
I realize—Canadian, American, English—
what an international delight I have ingested.
The world gathered
to give sustenance to my flesh.

I know,
I would be a giddy fool
to ignore each day's
daunting messages:
the old lady's weary glance,
the mortal horror
told by the road-kil ed man
etched into my psyche
by headlights,
the truth of
this ledger of days and days
of rote recitals
down to some sifting
drudge toward death.

I could strive for loftier answers—

philosophical forays into
spiritual essence,
but dusty tomes do little for me
to allay the fatigue of misery,
the frailty of flesh,
the near certainty
of our irrelevance.

And again,
the question: *Why the hell bother?*

I called home
and we said
a few funny words of love.
Then I stopped off
at the local McDonald's
for a drive-thru breakfast.

I pulled the car off down by the park.

An Egg McMuffin.

Yes.
There's the answer.

Assessing the Status of Our Longings

It occurs to me that we need a means of assessing the status of our longings.

What is honest healthy yearning that can inspire radical departure from the mundane toxins of daily toil? What draws us to paths of exceptional potential?

What is but maudlin pap that gums up our mechanisms of useful activity with sentimental distortions of a nonexistent past, shallow perceptions of the present, and delusional prophecies of the future?

How are we to determine which of the pangs that ache within the complex of our identity are signposts to superhighways of greater destiny—and which are but arrows directing us to cul-de-sacs of introspective stagnation?

And, most significantly, which are the road signs that accurately tell us where we are at this moment?

And the Path Goes On.
R. Nichols / 2017

Thanks for Reading My Book

Thanks for reading my book.

Without you this is just a conglomeration of introspective sketches and road-journa s.

I give them to you and the connection, the mutual embrace of art becomes possible.

Anc the Path Goes On

Appendix 1

A bit of commentary on the passing scene. Notation of money spent.

But they are much more than that. Collectively, they are a week's journey into being. I really can't tell you why these crude scraps are so important. But, on some primal level—the reason for the lives we live, the places we go, the people along our ways—it's a big deal.

Hitchhiking Trip from Woodbridge, Virginia, to Key West, Florida, 8:30 a.m., 8/4/62

1. Truck—South Hill, VA – Driving to ? (20 cents, food)

2. Station Wagon—from Conn., Near Apex, N.C. Very active—leaving wife, going to Australia.

3. Colored man, no teeth in front, watermelon truck—to Apex (food, 35 cents).

4. Straw Hat—Good Heavens, what a hick, to Tunstable Grocery—to New Hill.

5. Chevy Ranch Wagon—Big house—to near daddy-owned mansion, Sanford.

6. Colored man—classy—manner of speech—Dr.'s degree, to 15-501 cut off.

7. Banjo—55 Chevy.

8. Columbia, S.C.—Colored man—Conversation—Very enjoyable trip—push-button fancy Buick '47—shared peaches.

9. Convertible—2 mi.

Warning Ticket *("Walking on wrong side of road"*
from Deputy Bubba)—Stranded 4 hrs.

10. Deep, rounded voice—ha ha (a little happy) to
    Batesburg. (15 cents).

11. Augusta, Geo. Louisville—Ride offer to Fla. for money.

12. T-Bird 3 mi. walk 2 mi.

13. Truck to Wadley—After 3 hr, wait, 20 cents—2 hrs.

14. Cadillac to Folkston, Geo. 2 couples—sick music
    (country), people also sick.

15. Convertible to Jacksonville, *Fla!*—Walk through town
    looking for access to Rt. 1. Long walk.

16. Lifesaver—slept in car off and on—to Daytona Beach, Fla.

17. Skinny man in Rambler convert.—slept in back seat (very
    small) — to Melbourne.

18. Truck driver—carrying oil drums of chemicals—Brakes
    went out—to 441.

19. Pickup truck—spray painter (4.97/hr.) to city limits (Miami).

20. Paper route man—told of contrast in beach and inland
    highways. To Palmero Expressway.

    "Hitchhiking" warning ticket (hurrah!)

    Our first great disgrace—took bus through Miami.
    Miami to Homestead.

21. 2 Cubans to Islamorada—one here 8 mo. and other 2 mo.—
Spoke of Cuba and hate of Castro, going back.
    Saw Everglades and ocean, beautiful green water, straight
    road.

22. Man to Marathon.

23. Couple with '46 Plymouth and air boat (avocado pears)—to Key West, Fla.—greatest disappointment of trip—full of bars, drunks, & rude women.

24/25. Rides by old car and drunk man.
Spent night in boathouse on wharf behind Pier Bar.
(airboat couple's place).

26. Ride to Naval Air Base—long, hot day, hungry, miserable wait.

27. Ride back to Key West by sailor.
Greyhound Bus to Miami (cold water at Bus Terminal)
$4.60

Walk part of way out of town then bus to outskirts – 55 cents.

28. Ride by New Yorker and sailors.

29. Rode in convertible to W. Palm.

30. Turtle hunters with wine.

31. Negro to Ft. Pierce—talked of discrimination and moonshine.

32. Negro to ?. I drove—talked of his women—life ambition to teach.

33. Young guy in Ford going to take a placement test.

34. Ford Econoline Truck to Jacksonville—bus to airport after 42 block walk—Got Pat (Quinn's) Palm Leaf.

35. Rain! Short ride to filling station. Man there with son last heard to be in Alaska (in army or college).

36. Ride from Air Force with broken windshield wiper to Yulee.

37. 3 ½ hour wait—ride with young man—might come to D.C. to Kingston.

38. To lake house by mechanic—in an Austin Morris.

39. Truck driver to Brunswick.

40. Ignoramus over to Rt. 17.

41. Lovers with corpse in back seat to Naval pickup station.

Long wait 'til morning (approx. 4 hrs.)—slept in ruts of a side road—had to jump up out of way of car and drag Buddy—sports car, tried to run us over.

42. Fruit truck with old man and fat woman.

43. Southern-warped White to Savannah (nice enough, but sick—ordinary southerners).

Walked to bridge—stopped at fruit market. Negro boys—old I lady—bought beans, peaches, and apples—

44. Old man (nice) from south side of bridge to Ridgeland.

45. Ride with Florida resident (electrician, worked on reconditioning ships. Told of shooting hitchhikers, hitting Blacks in head, and running car full of Blacks into river. Also told of dragging at Daytona (165 mph/) to Charleston, N.C.

46. Stood next to swamp—miserable because of gnats—short ride to outskirts.

47. Resident going to D.C. (in few days—enjoyed talk—many subjects) to Wilmington, North Carolina.

Slept couple of hours in small park (hiding from road).

48. Caught ride from Marine in fast (129 mph) car—to Jacksonville, NC (Camp Lejeune).

   All night wait—sat in filling station—morning discussion with Buddy—flare up.

49. Long walk up the highway after Buddy—ride with bread truck—gave us rolls—reconnection with Buddy to New Burn.
   Walked across 2-mile bridge.

50. Ride with quiet guy (had to sit on left side of car because of shock absorber).

51. Boring ride to Norfolk—walked 4 mi. to Buddy's sister's trailer—good meal—1st good night's sleep—slept untill 12 the next morning.

52. Short rides to Suffolk—had to go south to catch #460.

53. Short ride through part of outskirts—talked with miserly filling-station attendant—he spoke of saving money— never hitchhiking (at 61).

54. Got us ride to Petersburg with man and dog.

55. Man with newspaper business

65. Ride to Richmond—walked through town—short ride to outskirts.

66. Ride to Ashland with three boys—wrestlers—big sour guys.

67. Radio DJ going to Maryland from Richmond.

68. Andy Boquette (classmate) to house.

Arrived 6:30 p.m. 8/11/62

Hattie Marie Ball
c. 1930

A long long way
from
Ball Fork/Scant
Branch,
Pinson Fork,
Kentucky.

Appendix 2

The Travel Journal
of
Hattie Marie Ball (Nichols)

I'll tell you about the California I had imagined. A few years ago I was going through boxes of family junk and treasure while cleaning out my dad's stuff. One box contained a mixture of old papers and photos and an album of souvenir cocktail napkins, ticket stubs and even some pressed flowers. Dad had told me Mom's nephew out in California had sent it to him a few years earlier. It was labeled "Hattie's stuff." Dad's only comment about the contents was something like, "It's just some junk from back before I knew her." When I finally dug through it I could see why Papa was less than thrilled to explore its contents. These were the artifacts of a Hattie Marie Ball that he hardly knew. As I shuffled through an era of her life that predated her forty-year tenure as "Penny" Nichols, wife to Robert Sr. and mother of John L., Nancy and Robert Jr. I came across an amazing document. In a single-spaced, elite-typed, four-page essay, my mother told of the trip she took from Roanoke, Virginia, to visit her sister Blandine in California in 1934.

As I read the delightful account of a twenty-six-year-old Pike County, Kentucky / Roanoke, Virginia girl's extended stay in the sunny spin of glamor and nature and a steady parade of suiters that was Los Angeles in the 1930s, it revealed a whole side of my sweet mother that I had only suspected by the gleam in her pretty blue eyes. My little mother of "Good Morning Glory" wake-up songs, afterschool cookies, and, "Good night, don't let the bed bugs bite," bedtime rituals was a wild thing in the days before she and Dad tied the knot. What a wonderful discovery.

I'm going to include the piece in its beautifully and spontaneously written entirety. Partially as a means of archiving a family treasure, but mostly so you can appreciate the spirit of those days in her life and the source of some of the wilder streaks in yours truly.

As you scan this freewheeling ramble through an adventure, remember a couple of things: 1. She was born the youngest of nine children up an Eastern Kentucky hollow called Ball Fork which split from Scant Branch, a tributary of the Pinson Fork River. Juxtapose that barefoot beginning with the writer of these words and it can make your mind spin. 2. Know that aside from playing a pretty lively ukulele and knowing every popular song from the '30s, there was little of any of this that we knew about—either me... or my sister or, apparently, our father.

My Trip to California—February 1934
Hattie Ball

As the old saying goes "A bad beginning—a good ending" so my trip began with a seven-hour delay due to heavy snow—to say the least was very discouraging. Once on my way things looked much brighter tho'—Travel was slow the first day. Took seven hours to reach Bristol, Tenn. had a five-minute change to another bus and proceeded on to Knoxville, Tenn. Arrived there at seven p.m.—spent the night at Hotel Farragut with the extravagance of $2.75 plus—took a bus at 6:45 next morning without breakfast, during the day we had several stops for lunch, tea, comfort etc., arriving in Memphis at 7:30 p.m.—had dinner with a big fat butter and egg man from Kansas City—well, anyway, I got a bus out of Memphis at 12:45 and my next change was in Dallas then the next change was El Paso, Texas, just a short stop and from there the bus came thru to L.A. just making the necessary stops to rest, eat— ETC. I might mention some of the 'gang' on the trip—who hailed from New York, Jersey, Boston, Indiana, Illinois—Harry was a big baseball player—Tony the Tally had high ambitions of being second to Babe Ruth—Dad was from Boston, the fatherly type who offered his assistance in case I got stranded in Los Angeles, then there was

Mr. Freeze, the lawyer with advice to the girl traveling alone—Phillip was an aviator stationed at the Naval Air Base and Coronado, Calif.—he was very interesting to talk to and had made the trip out several times and knew all the points of interest. Genevieve was just one of those girls with romantic ideas she thought it would be swell if I fell in love with Phillip and she could be the bridesmaid— the balance of the bunch was made up of the N.Y. Jewish Mama with a line of lingo that I could not comprehend.

Blandine and Verd met me at the L.A. station—we had a long ride before coming home—but when we finally arrived Verd just tried himself with a Gin Fizz—and Blandine had put herself out to the extent of a chicken dinner—Saturday night I met the gang and we went to a dance at the Rainbow Gardens—gorgeous ball room, approximately four thousand people there—swell time—Sunday, my first airplane ride—Bobby Givens, the donor—Blandine and Verd along. Then to Ocean Park and Venice Beach—the drive to the beach was beautiful. The following week to town shopping and to see the city—to Los Angeles Theatre—lunch at the "Arbor"— Friday night dance with Bobby—didn't get hi' but felt plenty good— after the dance to Givens' for eats and another little drink—home 3:30 a.m.—Sunday—drive thru Hollywood, Beverly Hills, Hollywood Hill, Westwood Hills—saw movie star homes, U.S.C. College, Coliseum where all the famous football games are played—saw the 110 mile per hour train that was out here on its first trip—then to Santa Monica Beach—a perfect "sunset" in the Pacific—a drive high up in the hills around L.A. to see the lighted city—too beautiful to describe—the vastness of it a l will get me down yet—Home, dinner at nine and tired. Another week of lazing around in the sunshine—in town a few times—also to Alhambra, Pasadena— and, by the way, I like Pasadena a lot—and I might say something about a bridge in Pasadena. It is a very beautiful drive across it and it must have a peculiar effect on people for more than a hundred persons have jumped to their destiny giving the name of "The Colorado Suicide Bridge." I was out with Verd one afternoon and he took me to see the Angelus Temple, but I am sorry to say I did not get a peek at the famous Aimee Semple MacPherson Hutton— Saturday Billie Givens spent the day with us and we prepared a picnic lunch for Sunday, but in the meantime we had to prepare an Italian Spaghetti dinner for Saturday night, the Givens and Bobby were here and that night Marshall & Frances Braun, Et Whitehead and her boyfriend came to see us so we had quite a nice party. Sunday we went to Tujunga (The home of Billie's sister) for our picnic. Tujunga is high in the foothills and the scene of the New Year's flood and also the recent forest fires, makes a picture to be remembered—went thru a very beautiful old castle—something very different from anything I have ever seen (hiked about 40 miles, it seemed to me) played bridge a while—ate the rest of the picnic—came home that night—had a wonderful time but tired—too much of a hike for an ole lady like me—stiff tomorrow. Monday, town shopping, show and lunch at Booze Bros., Rueben at eight—Tuesday, Bobby and I went to Long Beach, saw some of the earthquake ruins, big oil fields (in action) to the beach with all the trimmings—about an eighty-mile drive in all—Thursday, Blandine, Verd, Rueben and I went to Goldbergs to dance—and did we have fun boy 'o' boy—held that tiger—Friday, had dinner downtown with Rueben, went to see George White Scandals. Saturday morning—Billie, Verd and I went to see "Catherine the Great," Saturday had a date with Bobby and the four of us went to a party at the "Brauns" in Glendale—danced, had enough to drink and a good time—Bobby was spending the week end so we decided to sit up all night but "the ol' sleep bogus" got us about three-thirty. Sunday, we went to Oak Wilde in the Arroyo Seco Canyon then hiked up in the mountains—a beautiful place, so cool, quiet and restful with mountains so high on both sides only a glimpse of the sun here and there and the water sparkling clear as a crystal—an ideal place to camp and have picnics. Sunday night Bobby and I went to see "Roman Scandals" and "Wood Dame" (double feature) all and all would have been a perfect day if Blandine hadn't laid her glasses on a bench and Bobby hadn't stuck his elbow thru them—bang! goes $7.50. Monday night Rueben came by (surprise) but we danced, played ping-pong then went for a walk, or rather a run in the moon shine, more of a night for romance than a race but having a married couple along it turned out to be a race with Verd taking high honor. Tuesday night, dinner with Father and Haney and a show afterward. Wednesday sick with a cold. Rueben brought some gin and I tried to drown my troubles—results—got tight and did forget my cold while the effects were in force—With all the "Whitehead's" remedies I think I am going to live. Thursday, date with Bobby—went to Tujunga with Billie and Tommy to see Sue—they played cards but

Bobby and I went walking—the moon was so close up on those mountains it felt like I could almost touch it—we went to a little Mexican Beer Garden and heard 'real' cowboys singing (or maybe they weren't real) but was very exciting—drank some beer, back to Sue's and had more beer—maybe it was the beer, or maybe the moon but Bobby said if I was a 'hometown girl' he could go for me in a big way—He is very sentimental but I like him—Friday, went downtown all by myself—didn't get lost either—bought me a cute white suit—yes, think I'll like it—hope my cold gets better so I can wear it Sunday—we had Rueben for dinner—a nice quiet evening at home UNTIL about eleven when we took a little stroll to the liquor store for gin and after that Verd wanted to play his cornet all night but we finally convinced him that we had to live in this neighborhood the next day and didn't want too much company (the neighbors). Saturday, Blandine is a good doctor but does not seem to be able to conquer this cold. Letter from the "Shaws" telling me I could stay as long as I wanted—business must be bad (or maybe I am just not important enough to be needed on the job) made me very happy for I do want to stay a little longer—Saturday night, a little party at home—Bobby brought me beautiful Easter flowers, more flowers from the Whiteheads—now don't I rate. Rueben came by to see how the cold was—didn't know he was coming—very good thank you, think I will have Pneumonia tomorrow—but he couldn't stay for I had a date and we were having other company—Grandma Whitehead served delicious apple pie and coffee later in the evening—Thomas and Kay had gotten a 'lover's quarrel' settled and were back in the fold. Just gotta be feeling better, for tomorrow is a big day. Tomorrow—Sunday, CATALINA—We left from the Whitehead's at eight o'clock and crove to Wilmington Harbor where we took the boat—and what a day—I think I was as near paradise today as I ever hope to be on this earth—I'll try to make myself clear, however, I cannot put down in words the beauty of the day. I am not poet enough—nor can I find words that would express or describe— justly—the beautiful trip we took—to my way of thinking, Catalina should rightly be called "Paradise Island." Immediately after landing we took the glassbottom boat trip over the Marine Gardens which is located in the bottom of the ocean—in this garden are various kinds of sea plants, shells, rock formations to say nothing about the variety of fish—one very interesting thing was a starfish clinging to the rocks—another unusual thing was what is called the

"Cucumber" –This cucumber is a green peculiar looking thing 96% vegetarian and 4% animal life—then we went on to the Seal Garden—and golly, such flocks of seals you cannot imagine, well, anyway, after the glass bottom boat trip we were all just about hungry enough to enjoy a full sized meal—had lunch at the Grille Café—after lunch we were off to the bird farm—and what beautiful birds to say nothing of the scenic bus trip there and back—just impossible to picture the beautiful settings around those California places—just must be seen to be appreciated. Took pictures, went thru the famous Casino and this is the most unusual building and has what is known as the "perfect" dance hall and what I mean it is perfect—of course, we went thru the Spanish Patio and one sees just about every kind of trinket that could be imagined in curio shops to say nothing of the Wide Brim Guitar Players—I mean the entertainers—this might not sound like doing much, but it took all of our day—Oh yes, we went to St. Catherina's Hotel and it is noted for its beauty—not much for the building but the grounds and the way it is nestled in one corner of the island, but if you want your heart to swell about three times its size just wait until you start to leave—romantic, gosh, one sure needs their 'best lover' along to help enjoy this end of a perfect day—After the first whistle blows, the band starts playing and, oh boy, oh boy, you just think you will die—honestly, you feel that you never want to say another word—just drink it all in and never get over the feelin'—then as the boat slowly leaves the band follows right along clear to the end of the pier playing "Farewell to Thee"—of course, at that hour (6:30 p.m.) the whole island is lighted up and I'm tellin' you it's a picture that lingers on and on—Whoever thought of the slogan "In all the world, no trip like this' expressed it just right. Now I must tell you something about the gorgeous boat trip over and back—Do you get the idea you are going to Europe, or do you, maybe it's just because I was from the country, but I thought it was heavenly—a real peppy orchestra and a 'plenty peppy bunch'—dancing all the way over and back—You would just fold your sides up laughing when the whole bunch would pile up together when the boat would rock from one side to the other, however, some were folding up for other reasons—never saw so many folks enjoying the same feeling in all my life (and I can truthfully say that I never felt the slightest bit sea sick). Takes 2½ hours each way—Following a week of many miseries, cold, sore throat, etc.—went to a dance at Wilsons' on

Thursday night—Rueben, Verd and Blandine—Oh, yes, I almost forgot we went thru the beautiful Biltmore Hotel and Verd must have been feeling his best for he could see no reason why we could not dance there since we were so terrible dressed up—it only cost $25 per for the evening, however, after much coaxing we compromised by going to "Wilson's", but even tho' it was not equal to the Biltmore we had just a bag full 'o' fun—Friday night Bobby came home with Verd and, of course, spent the night—didn't go out. Saturday night we went on a camping trip, and what I mean it was a real camping trip in the beautiful Arroyo Seco Canyon—Tommy's birthday party—Tommy, Billie, Verd, Blancine, Bobby and myself—had a cute cabin "Silver Brook" with four beds, a wood stove, table, chairs etc., just as comfy as home—went to a dance at Oak Wilde Tavern just in our camping clothes and gotta kick out of doin' that—after we came back to camp we built a fire, made coffee, sandwiches and ate gobs—to bed late—up early for a five-mile hike up thru the canyon—impossible to describe the beauty and the huge difference in those mountains and the ones of Ol' Virginia—but will say this— it was the most thrilling hike I ever took—if you can picture goats trying to pass on the corner of a cliff you can get some idea of this trail along the edge of those ledges that are straight up and down— and what I mean you have to keep your nerves pretty well under control in case a snake or lizard happens to run between your feet for they do just that sometimes, fact is, it really happened—Bobby killed one snake and caught the other to bring home but after carrying if for miles by the tail he was informed it was a $100.00 fine to catch that type for they kept the rattlesnakes killed, well anyway, everyone was plenty tired and poor Tommie being a famous "rubber" gave everyone a rub-down and we had a nap before eating—but when we did eat, we ate plenty—cleaned the cabin and checked out, but we didn't leave—went to the tavern and played pool and other games and enjoyed the sights around before leaving—All good things must come to an end and I'm sorry to say but my vacation is over and now I must pack to go home, but with all the fun I have had I guess I have nothing to crab about—I am just happy that I have had—one perfect vacation—in my life and that will mean a lot even when I am an old lady and I'll have something to tell my grandchildren.

By the time I read these words Mom was over twenty years passed. But, yes, my Dear Mother, you really had a perfect vacation to tell us about. I'm so proud of my mother, not only that she was such a spirit in her younger days, but also that she was able to so thoroughly express her experiences. My mama could really write! But probably, most of all, I love how deeply affected she was by the wonders of the world through which she passed. I know just how she felt.

Notes

Paths
They Spoke with Filth and Beauty

Part I: The Travel Path

You Won't Know Anything (2016)
Notes from an Early Journey (1962 / ed. 2017)
> So it started, Robert and his magic and sometimes not so magical thumb out upon the highways giving motion and substance to the metaphor of life's path.

Next Year We'll Go North (1962)
It Was a Long Road (1962)
Hitchhiking South (1962)
I Saw Life Yesterday (1962)
The Road Path Continues (collected from various years 1968-2017)
> The primary source of the chapters about my mid-sixties travel is twenty pages of single-spaced recollection I wrote during the summer of 1968. Carol, with much eye strain, profanity, and persistence, transcribed this faded document into MS Word copy. She's a better editor than I. To my pleasant surprise, much of the writing held up pretty well. What appears here is edited for typos and continuity. To the original text I added sections, corrections, and entire chapters written in 2016-2017.

A Short and Serious Talk (collected from various years 1968-2017)
A Dream Actualizes
Hitchhiking Trip
"You Ain't No Preacher, Are You?"
Sleep in an Eroded Field
Inching and Quarter-Inching
A Girl in Southern Missouri
A Hard Road Onward
The Exterminator
Just Some Good Ol' Boys
Kansas and the Wind
The Dogman

The Rubber-man
Denver...
The Bus to Cheyenne
From the Infinite to California
Welcome to California
Rest and Redetermination in Glendale (2017)
California Bleeding
A Night at the Ritz
Letter to Carol
The Motorcycle
I Didn't Buy the Flashy Helmet
Bob and Alvin Lackey (2017)
U.S. 199 (2017)
Rescue (2017)
The Way Home (2017)
The Nature of a Pure Gift (2017)
Notes from an Old Man's Journey (2017)

Part II: Some More Travel, People, and Places

A Poem—Never Written (Excerpt from a June 26, 1971, journal entry.
     Train from Hanover to Lubeck, Germany.)

Taiwan Sketches (1986)

Taipei Morning
Travel Sketch: Taipei to Hualien
Unfinished, Un-mailed Letter
Snake Alley and the Red-Light Ladies
The Buddha-Man
... And

No Words. Only Heart. (2003)
     Carol, Kristin, and I took an amazing trip to Peru in 2003. The
     catacombs beneath the ancient cathedral in Lima (thousands of
     skulls and leg bones and all); the Incan center of the earth—
     Cusco (11,000 feet up into the Andes where Kristin developed a
     real liking for the coca tea dispensed freely in the lobby of the
     hotel as a remedy for effect of the high altitude); the train trip to
     Aguas Calientes; Machu Picchu; and... my solitary trek up the
     sacred mountain, Huayna Picchu (a spirit journey that resounds
     in all the days since).

Dancing With the Gods (2012)
    It's all a holy sacred wonder to me.

Roatán / December 2005 (2006)
  The Sea
  Captain Emerald's Craft
  Rain, Cheese Quesadillas
  End

Part III: Darkness along the Path
    Wouldn't it be nice if we didn't have to tell the whole (and "hole")
    truth? Racism—man, what a blight upon our culture.
The Color of Reality (2017)
A Man Died That Night: Old Miss Riots
Summer, 1963 (1963)
The Hole Truth (c. 2004)
True Times (1974)
Casual Jokes of Hatred (1999)
Slumber Station (2016)
2017 Update on Racism (2017)

Part IV: Other Views of the Path

Paths
Just a Traveler
Days upon the Highway (song, 1984)
The Street-Man (2014)
A Sad Little Girl (1987)
Sweet Scene on a Downtown Sidewalk (1988 / ed. 2017)
Scene from the City (2014 / ed. 2016)
Silhouette-Man Passing (1990s / ed.2015)
Beggar-Man and the Blessing of the Child (c. 2000 / 2015)
Captive at a Fast Food Café (1989)
Oasis Beside the Rolling Road
The Old Boys
Finish
Denver Bus Terminal (1977 / 1980s)
I Saw the Clipping
    Of course, "Georgie" had a real name, as did he have a real life,
    and… let him rest in peace.
A Visit Downtown (1963 / ed. 2015)

Old Man and the Twisted Metal (c. 1978 / ed 2017)
Sam (1969 / 2017)
It Is an All-Cowboy Music Night (1989 / 2016)
He Might Have Been Joking (c. 2004)
Inclusion (c. 2002 / ed. 2017)
The Two Girls in the Next Booth
Washer-Man (c. 2010)
Oh, My Goodness (2014 / 2016)
Girl Playing in the Ocean (2004 / 2017)
Red Sneakers (2075 /2017)
A Dark Little Baby (1974 / ed. 2014)
The Farmer (2016)
The Factory Ladies' Reunion (c. 2009)
I Caught the Glance (c. 2009 / ed. 2016)
Whispered (c. 1974 / ed. 2016)
Assessing the Status of Our Longings
Thanks for Reading My Book
Appendix 1
Hitchhiking Trip from Woodbridge, Virginia, to Key West,
     Florida, 8:30 a.m., 8/4/62

Appendix 2
     The Travel Journal of Hattie Marie Ball (1934)

Other Works by Robert Nichols

Most of these titles are currently published as e-Books available through all the major distributors—Kindle, Nook, etc. Also, printed editions are in process as books-on-demand, I will get them out—hey, it's a lot of work.

Books etc.

The Kristin Book (1987)

Story of the first fifteen years of the life of my daughter who was born with Down Syndrome.

This book, reissued with an update, is now available in eBook format as ***The Kristin Book: Update 2013***

Take the Aspen Train (1988)

Co-authored with Edward Larsh. Coffee table, Colorado history / social philosophy / train book. *(No longer available.)*

Adventures in the High Wind (1990)

Collection of my poems, stories, and essays.
eBook edition, 2013.

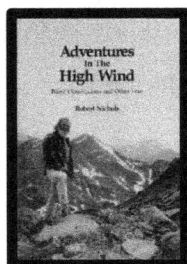

Leadville, U.S.A (1993)

Co-authored with Edward Larsh. Oral history of Leadville, Colorado. *(No longer available.)*

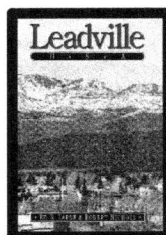

The High Priest of Hallelujah (1999)

Niche-less novel of poetic vision. humor, and satire.
eBook edition, 2015.

Summer Words, 2000 (2001)

Collection of short essays about laughter, God, knife throwing and much more.
e-Book edition, 2014.

The Booklets (2001 and...)

12-14 page booklets of poetry, short stories, essays—you know: literature. Currently there are five of these little gems published with more to come. Some day...

The Five Great Truths of Uncle Bob (2002)

A culminating work of philosophy, religion, and practical wisdom (and all on one side of a sheet of paper).

God of the Poets (2003)

It took me twenty years to get this one right. When I finished the first version in '83 I didn't know enough to write my own novel. Perhaps now I do. I was pretty much just a stenographer for the real author, God. This isn't traditional stuff. It's a story of art, love, humanity and... *the purpose of life*.
e-Book edition, 2014.

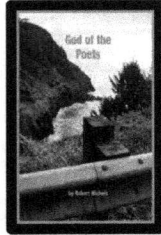

Albatross: The Curse of Honesty (2013)

The first novel I wrote, and re-wrote, and finally published. It's a funny and touching tale of a fellow whose life is nearly destoyed by the curse of absolute honesty.

The Great Book of Bob (2009)
The Great Book of Bob **eBook edition** (2014)

A unified collection of humorous, soul-wrenching, and harshly honest tales and thoughts gleaned from a lifelong love story— stories of a poet's love of sunrises, poetic epiphanies, laughter, and for the soulmate of his life. And the best part about it, it's not some icky-sticky, lovey-poo bunch of hearts and flowers. It's hard-edged wonder and real reason for all of us to be glad to be alive. I tell *my* stories that we may each realize the significance of our own.

Uncle Bob's Big Book of Happy (2017)

I should make this clear from the start. None of this is easy. The first chapter of this work starts out saying exactly that: This will not be easy. I tell some hard truths. Don't be misled by the mirthful lilt of my title. Uncle Bob here will do his best to help you be happy, but none of this means diddly-squat if you can't face harsher aspects of our everyday journey. I write this book in hopes that my stories, theories, blathering bilge and sublime prayers may be of help to you in avoiding the burden, the curse of bitterness. It's no fun living in a world of bitchy whiners, angry jerks, and cranky bastards. You know what I mean.

THE FOOTLOCKER SERIES

This is a series of eBooks gleaned from fifty years of writing excavated from Robert Nichols' old footlocker of notebooks and scraps of papers—the repository of a life of art.

For information contact Robert Nichols at Mtmuse44@aol.com.

Titles:

about Time
about Mountain Living
about Seasons
about Paths

about Time: Poems and Other Stories (2015)

The first in the series—poetry, stories, and photography about ancient time, the time of children, the time of young adults, and the time of growing old. It's really not about time at all. This is a book about life.

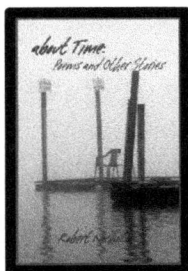

about Mountain Living: Finding a Way (2015)

A journey told in story and poem. A life trek from discontent and restlessness to commitment and discovery. This work tells of a succession of habitats and lifestyles progressing farther and farther from the city and further into a better destiny—from apartment to cabin to tipi to hilltop shrine of art, nature, and spirit. A journey from complacent certainty to out-on-the-edge primal survival. Perhaps my story will encourage yours. And, beyond the tale I tell, just read the poems and stories as the art they are intended to be. You will laugh and weep and contemplate—you will be changed.

about Seasons: the Wind and Weather of Our Days (2016)

Poems of the seasons—not just some cliché sweetness about leaves and blossoms either. This is the core stuff of being. Seasons, wind, and weather—the fierce and beautiful power of Nature that can keep us humble and exhilarated throughout our lives. It is the very "life and death" intensity of these metamorphic cycles that excites the turning of our years with risk and wonder. Time takes away our days, storms wash away our safety, seasons etch our flesh with danger. Old Spirits out on the plains once told me, "Earth shall never be tame... celebrate your fear and feel you are alive!" Yes!

Robert. March afternoon. 2017

www.ingramcontent.com/pod-product-compliance
Lightning Source LLC
Chambersburg PA
CBHW060738050426
42449CB00008B/1266